THE HULL WHALING TRADE

An Arctic Enterprise

by

Arthur G. Credland

HUTTON PRESS
1995

Published by

The Hutton Press Ltd.,
130 Canada Drive, Cherry Burton,
Beverley, East Yorkshire, HU17 7SB

Printed and bound by

Clifford Ward and Co. (Bridlington) Ltd.,
55 West Street, Bridlngton,
East Yorkshire YO15 3DZ

*There is a Leviathanic Museum, they tell me in Hull,
England, one of the whaling ports of the country, where they
have some fine specimens of fin-backs and other whales...*

*Moreover at a place in Yorkshire, England, Burton Constable
by name, a certain Sir Clifford Constable has in his possession
the skeleton of a Sperm Whale.*

Herman Melville, *Moby Dick*, 1851.

ISBN 1 872167 73 X

CONTENTS

ACKNOWLEDGEMENTS

The basis for any detailed investigation of the Hull whaling trade rests firmly on the outstanding collections of documents, paintings and artefacts in the Town Docks Museum. Some of these items were given to the Literary and Philosophical Society in the last century by the local whaleship owners and whaling masters as well as Arctic explorers such as Sir John Ross, but the majority have been received from their descendants. Many individuals have also shared information they have gleaned while researching the lives of their forebears and a special thank you must go to Philip Hepton for his important work on the Wells family and the last years of Hull whaling.

An outstanding visual record is provided by the splendid paintings by local artists and indeed the strong local tradition of marine painting largely derives from the boom years of the Arctic fishery. The pride of the shipowners and masters in their vessels led to an increasing demand for ship portraits and humble signwriters and artisans were transformed into artists as a result. Thomas Fletcher, who is the earliest ship portrait painter recorded in Hull, was a ship painter in the literal sense and organised his workmen to daub ships' timbers with their paint mops and tar brushes. He is represented by a more than competent picture of the *Molly and Friends*, commissioned by Angus Sadler who had been master of the former vessel between 1796-1802; so far this is the only canvas from his hand which has been identified. Fletcher was followed by Robert Willoughby a prolific painter of whaleship portraits. They were usually simple compositions, a profile and a stern view but he executed a magnificent canvas of Samuel Cooper's fleet on 1803, which measures fifty-five by seventy-two inches, and shows five vessels, each in two views. Then followed John Ward (1798-1849) Hull's greatest marine artist of the nineteenth century. His whaling scenes are some of the finest ever produced and the convincing representation of icebergs and floes, quite unlike the fluffy sugar candy of Willoughby, strongly suggests that Ward had actually visited the Arctic to study the landscape at first hand.

The majority of the illustrations are from the Town Docks Museums's own collections but we should like to thank Sir Anthony Wagner, the late Mrs. P. A. Tritton, Mrs. S. J. Humphries, Mr. R. P. Langton, Mr. M. K. Lister, the Wardens and Brethren of the Hull Trinity House, Winnipeg Archive Service, Philadelphia Maritime Museum, the Kendall Whaling Museum, Sharon, Mass., and the Dundee City Museum for permission to reproduce items in their possession.

I am further indebted to Capt. Clements Markham Colbeck for details of the career of his father Capt. William Colbeck.

Special thanks are due also to the staff of the Hull City Archives, the Local History Library, Albion Street, and my colleagues in the Hull Museum and Art Gallery Service for their able assistance. The former Curator, Mr. John Bradshaw has encouraged the project and Mr. Graham Edwards of our design staff has prepared many of the photographs. Miss Jayne Karlsen, Mrs. Anne Lamb and Miss Dorothy Soulsby have all been involved in producing a readable typescript translated from my illegible scrawl!

Arthur G. Credland
Town Docks Museum
February 1995

INTRODUCTION
THE ORIGINS OF EUROPEAN WHALING

The origins of organised whaling in Europe have yet to be determined in detail, but the Basques of the French and Spanish coast had certainly established a shore-based industry before the twelfth century. For hundreds of years the bounty of a whale accidentally stranded on the shore was much appreciated by the local inhabitants who would utilise its meat, oil and bone to the full. Excavation of the neolithic settlement of Skara Brae, Orkney revealed a number of cetacean remains. Small tail vertebrae had been hollowed out for holding pigments and larger examples made into basins or bowls. A number of whale jawbones seem to have served as roof supports as was often the case in the semi-subterranean houses of the Eskimo on the Greenland coast.

The Franks casket in the British Museum is made up of carved plaques of skeletal whalebone handsomely decorated with a mixture of classical and biblical subjects, including Romulus and Remus and the siege of Jerusalem. It was produced in a Northumbrian workshop of the eighth century A.D. and an inscription indicates that the bone came from a stranded whale. A group of chessmen found at Wimborne, Dorset, made of whalebone, probably in the tenth century, are also fine examples of Anglo-Saxon craftsmanship. All these artefacts were made from raw materials taken from the larger types of whale such as the Right Whale, Sperm Whale and various species of rorqual for which there is no real evidence of organised pursuit in the early middle ages or prehistory. Coastal strandings were and still are a frequent event, even now when the stocks of most species have been diminished by over exploitation.

There is good evidence for seal-hunting and the pursuit of porpoises and pilot whales during the Scandinavian Mesolithic and rock carvings of pilot whales in southern Norway indicate familiarity with this species in the Stone age.

We have documentary evidence from the late sixteenth century for the *grindhrap* or whale drive of the Faroes, a custom which persists to this day. Large schools of pilot whales are driven ahead of a squadron of small boats until they come ashore and can be slaughtered wholesale in the shallows. Similar whale drives took place in Shetland into the early part of the twentieth century and such a basic technique would have been well within the capabilities of prehistoric man.

The walrus was considered by our ancestors to be a type of whale indeed the name (A-S *horshwael*; Icelandic *hross-hvalr*) literally means whale-horse. Their tusks provided a source of ivory which became more and more important as the supply of elephant ivory declined with the collapse of the Roman empire. Morse (walrus) ivory was used in increasing quantities and traded throughout the markets of Europe. The chessmen made sometime in the middle of the twelfth century by a Scandinavian craftsman and discovered in Lewis were all made from walrus ivory as were many of the altar crosses, crozier heads and combs of the early middle ages.

In the late ninth century Ohthere, a Norwegian traveller and merchant, presented a pair of walrus tusks to King Alfred and this probably marks the beginning of regular shipments into England. Ohthere described to the King and his court the long journeys he had made up the Norwegian coast and into the White Sea in search of ivory and other valuable commodities.

Walrus hide provided a useful material for making a very tough rope, by skinning it spiral fashion from the tail, much like the Eskimo uses the seal to provide himself with lines for his harpoons. In nineteenth century England walrus hide was tanned to make the drive belts which were so essential to the mills of those days. Each machine would take its power from a steam engine or water wheel through a belt and pulley connected to the drive shaft. The Hull firm of J. H. Fenner advertised as

Muscovy company whaling bark of 70 tons c.1610.

Series of vignettes of walrus hunting as conducted at the Spitzbergen fishery based on a series of watercolours painted by Robert Fotherby in a journal aboard a Muscovy company ship in 1613.

The Seamorce is in quantity as bigg as an oxe

When the whale is killed hee is in this manner towed to the shipps by twoe or three shal: lops made fast one to another.

The peeces of blubber are towed to the shore side by a shallop and drawne on shore by a crane or caried by twoe menn on a barrowe to y twoe cutters w which cutts them the breadt of a trencher and very thine eche by twoe boyes or caried to handhooks to y chopers

Thus they make cleane and scrape y whale fins

A tent and Coopers at worke

472 A Whale is ordinarly about 60 foote longe

When the whale comes aboue water y shallop rowes towards him and being within reach of him the harpoiner darts his harpingiron at him out of both his hands and being fast they lance him to death

The whale is cut up as hee lyes floting crosse the sterne of a shipp the blubber is cut from the flesh by peeces 3 or 4 foote long and being rased is rowed on shore towards the coppers

They place 2 or 3 coppers on a rve and y chopping boate on the one side and the coolling boate on the other side to receaue y oyle of y coppers, the chopt blubber being boyled is taken out of the coppers and put in wicker baskets or barowes wherin the oyle is dreaned and runes into y cooler w it falls water out of w it is conuaied by troughes into buts of casel

The manner of killing y Seamorces

Flensing a whale drawn onto the shore using a windlass. This was probably the usual method in the Biscay fishery during the Middle Ages.

'tanners and manufacturers of the famous patent *walrus hide strapping*, now used in the principal works in the Kingdom', a product they had patented in 1855.

The venturing voyages of the later middle ages plotted new territory on the map and gathered knowledge of the great resources of fish, whales and walrus waiting to be exploited in the north Atlantic and the Arctic. One of the spurs to these brave leaps into the unknown was the closure of many of the overland trade routes into Europe from the east owing to the expansion of the Turkish Empire in the fifteenth century. At the same time the sea routes by the Cape of Good Hope and the Magellan Straits were monopolised by the Portuguese and Spanish. Thus began the search for the elusive north-west passage to give Britain undisputed access to the oriental spice trade.

Frobisher made his first northern voyage in 1576 and John Davis penetrated the strait named after him in 1585 while Hudson between 1607-11 further expanded our knowledge of the north American coastline. Baffin pushed even further north in 1615 and Luke Fox, born in St. Mary's parish, Hull, in 1586, explored the channel which still bears his name after sailing from Bristol in 1631 under the patronage of Charles I. Illusory as the north west passage proved to be the geographical knowledge accumulated by these intrepid sailors encouraged the eventual exploitation of the untapped resources of the Arctic.

European whaling, as we have seen, was firmly established in the Bay of Biscay during the Middle Ages but the severe decline in numbers of migrating Biscay Right Whales caused the Basques to look further afield for new whaling grounds. During the sixteenth and seventeenth centuries a number of shore stations were set

Dutch whalers at the Spitsbergen fishery. An oil painting by Abraham Storck (1644-1710), in the collections of the Prins Hendrick Museum, Rotterdam.

up along the strait of Belle Isle, the narrow channel separating Newfoundland from mainland Canada. A brave venture this ultimately failed because of the vast distances involved which had to be negotiated by the tiny sailing vessels (200 tons and often much less) which were available at this period. They voyaged across the north Atlantic with all the hazards of fog, icebergs and gales to bring home the precious cargo to France and Spain. It was, however, the Dutch who were the first to exploit whale stocks on a large scale away from home waters. Initially employing Basque harpooners, to learn from them the skills of the whale hunt, the Dutch dominated the Spitsbergen fishery throughout the seventeenth century exploiting extensive populations of the Greenland Right Whale, a larger relative of the Biscay animal, up to sixty feet long and weighing as many tons. Called the 'bay fishery' because the prey was caught close inshore, or within the deep fjords which indent the Spitsbergen coast, many nations vied for a share in the rich resource though the English, Germans and Danes came off a poor second to the Dutch. Their huge fleet, no less than 246 vessels in 1684, was able to supply the whole of Europe with all the oil and whalebone (baleen) they were likely to need. Britain imported these products from Amsterdam even while the attempts to establish a thriving native industry were at their height. These efforts foundered on the rivalries between the various east coast ports and the determination of the Muscovy company in London to establish a monopoly. They regarded all other whalers as 'interlopers' and were constantly in dispute with the men of Hull and Yarmouth whom they accused of 'trespassing' in northern waters.

Hull vessels were sailing up to Vardo (called Wardhouse by the British), at the northern tip of the Scandinavian peninsular, in the latter part of the sixteenth century. These were probably trading voyages at first but Bear Island, discovered by Barents in 1594, was visited by Sir Francis Cherie in 1603 and the populations of walrus attracted considerable attention. Reports of cod fish and whale oil brought into Hull from Wardhouse voyages

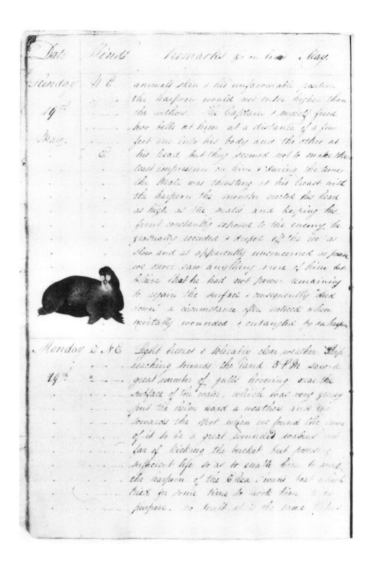

*Page from the log of the whaleship **Abram**, 1839. Walrus were still being hunted by the nineteenth century whalers but this was subsidiary to their efforts in catching whales and seals.*

indicate the gradual development of these northern sea fisheries. When ships were small, navigation instruments primitive and maps unreliable a route following the Norwegian coast before striking off to Bear Island and Spitsbergen was the safest to follow. As knowledge of these distant waters increased vessels invariably made the direct passage northwards.

It was the Englishman Henry Hudson, in the employment of the Muscovy company, who rediscovered Spitsbergen in 1607 previously sighted by the Dutchman William Barents, and the men of Hull were among the first to prosecute the whale fishery there. Hudson also discovered at the same time the island between Spitsbergen and Greenland later called Jan Mayen after Jan May of Schellinkhout who reached it in 1611. Generally known to the British as Trinity Island it is said to have been granted as a fishing station to the Hull Corporation in 1618 following a petition to James I during the protracted fight against the Muscovy company's monopoly.

Thomas Marmaduke, a brother of the Hull Trinity House, was one of the great names of these pioneering days in the northern seas. He was at Bear Island in the summer of 1609 in command of the *Heartsease* and then sailed north for Spitsbergen, only the third person to visit there after Barents and Hudson. He was there again in 1611, walrus hunting, when he rescued the crews of two Muscovy Company vessels which had been wrecked. He made the first considerable exploration of the north coast in 1612, and established such a reputation as a navigator that he was engaged in 1613 and 1614 by the Muscovy Company. Previously he had sailed on his own account and like all the other independent masters had been regarded as an 'interloper' in the company's preserves. He was one of the first men to sight Jan Mayen island and indeed claimed to have discovered it and this is no doubt why the men of Hull were granted its fishery by the King though with a Dutch presence already firmly established this was little more than a gesture.

Hull whaling continued during the Civil War and Launcelot Anderson master of the *Whale* returned home in 1643 whilst the town, which was a parliamentary stronghold, was under siege by Royalist forces. Anderson was master of the whaling ship which, in May 1631, rescued eight whalers who had been left behind on Spitsbergen and were the first Englishmen to winter there. In a manuscript preserved in the British Museum he claims to have made no less than thirty-three voyages to the Greenland fishery.

The Dutch increased their grip on the northern fishery, though the Navigation Acts which restricted the employment of foreign ships in the nation's external trade gave some consolation to the native enterprise. The Anglo-Dutch wars of 1652-4, 1665-7 and 1672-4 which resulted from these enactments led to no decisive conclusion between the two contending navies and Holland remained as strong as ever as a trading nation. At the close of the century British whaling was moribund and Hull's 'Greenland house' built in 1674 at the joint expense of the local merchants was being used to store corn and general merchandise.

CHAPTER 1
HULL WHALING IN THE SIXTEENTH TO EIGHTEENTH CENTURIES

Despite the simple technology, pursuit in a whaleboat followed by harpooning and lancing, the presence of the huge Dutch fleet as well as the English, French, Danes and Germans resulted in a drastic depletion of the stocks of whales. The bay fishery was abandoned soon after 1670 and the whalers then sought their prey offshore in the seas west of Spitsbergen and along the east coast of Greenland. Now instead of boiling the raw blubber on shore it was merely chopped into pieces small enough to pass through the bung hole of the barrels and brought home to be processed. The Dutch pioneered the Davis Strait fishery in the eighteenth century but these new grounds were not extensively explored by the British till the early nineteenth century when the Netherlands involvement in whaling had ceased.

The foundations for the great flowering of the city's whaling trade were laid by James Hamilton, a Hull merchant who traded extensively with the eastern seaboard of America. He had begun to import oil, product of the colonial whaling trade which had developed during the 1730's chiefly out of Nantucket and Rhode Island. Supplies were, however, interrupted by the effects of French expansionism so Hamilton, in 1754, responded to the loss of lucrative business by equipping his own vessel, the *York*, for a voyage to Greenland. His example was followed by Joseph and Robert Pease, William Turner and Samuel Dewitt and the Hull Whale Fishery company was floated with a capital of £20,000. A government bounty paid to encourage the growth of the industry was set at forty shillings per ship ton in 1750, a total of some six hundred pounds sterling for each vessel, and this must have provided additional incentive for the venture.

The Peases were major oil-importers from Holland and they had an established office and counting house in Amsterdam. William Turner was not only the largest whalebone importer in Hull but perhaps in the whole of Britain whilst Dewitt was a Dutch sea captain and merchant. The men involved in this revival of the local whaling interest were therefore all involved in the oil and bone trades traditionally enjoyed with Holland, but latterly with North America.

The end of hostilities and the resumption of supplies from the colonies as well as the effects of war in Europe combined to stifle this piece of local enterprise. After three years when no vessels sailed to Greenland the imposition of duty on oil and bone from the colonies gave a fresh impetus and Samuel Standidge fitted out the *Berry*. Previously belonging to the Hull Whale Fishery company she brought back for her owner the produce of one whale and several hundred seal skins. The *Britannia* and *British Queen* were added to the fleet and others joined in the trade so that by 1775 a fleet of twelve ships was sailing to Greenland from Hull though the onset of the Revolutionary war and the trade depression which resulted soon reduced numbers to a mere three or four ships a season.

The Dutch presence in the Greenland fishery was massive in the eary eighteenth century reaching an all time peak of 1494 sailings in 1744! In 1789 there were still over five hundred departures for the fishery but the naval wars with England 1780-4 and particularly the long blockade of the Netherlands during the French domination, 1795-1813, effectively killed off this already languishing trade. Competition from the British and the development of whaling in America had begun this decline so that by 1798 only nine vessels were left in the fleet. This and the collapse of the American industry in 1784 combined to make possible the foundation of Hull's pre-eminence so that by the end of the century local vessels comprised about 40% of the British participants in the trade.

The chief quarry in the waters between Spitsbergen and Greenland and later in the Davis Strait fishery remained

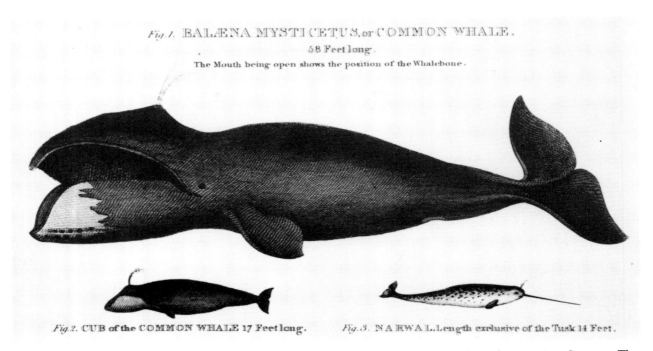

Fig.1. BALÆNA MYSTICETUS, or COMMON WHALE.

58 Feet long.

The Mouth being open shows the position of the Whalebone.

Fig.2. CUB of the COMMON WHALE 17 Feet long.   *Fig.3.* NARWAL. Length exclusive of the Tusk 14 Feet.

Greenland Right Whale, Balaena mysticetus, which can grow up to sixty feet long and weigh some sixty-five tons. The blubber, eight to twenty-four inches thick, accounts for between one fifth and one half of the total weight and each ton yields three quarters of a ton of oil. Reproduced from William Scoresby **An Account of the Arctic Regions,** *1820.*

the Greenland Right Whale. Each of these huge animals could provide up to a ton of bone and twenty tons of oil. Prices of course fluctuated but oil was usually sold for between £20 and £50 a ton. Since the sixteenth century the biggest demand for oil had come from the soapmakers but later it was used extensively for lamp fuel until replaced by colza (rape) oil and paraffin during the second half of the nineteenth century. The oil was much used in the leather industries and by textile manufacturers for softening coarse woollen cloths. A tradition of whalebone (baleen) cutting and stay-making helped create an appetite for this material which in the eighteenth century could not be satisfied by the local fleet. In 1775 for example 17,472lb of whalebone were brought coastwise to Hull from Whitby and Scarborough though

a significant proportion of this was probably traded on to London and the larger centres of population inland.

The thriving state of Hull's maritime activities emphasised the need for improved dock facilities in the port. Ever since the middle ages the only place where vessels could load and unload their cargoes was at the staithes between the mouth of the river Hull and the North Bridge, a stretch of water which became known as the 'old harbour' or haven. Finally after much agitation and the formation of the Hull Dock company the town's first enclosed dock was open to shipping on the 22 August 1778. A whaleship was the first vessel to enter which is an indication of the esteem in which the Greenland trade was held at this time. The *Manchester* of Messrs. Staniforth and Ramsey was decorated overall with the flags of the

An eighteenth century print of the Greenland fishery.
Note the exceptionally long 'mik' or crotch, in which the shaft of the harpoon is rested,
on the starboard side of the whaleboat. The boatsteerer is standing up to manage
the long steering oar. Until the boat is near enough for an attack the harpooner sits on his bench and works the bow oar.

nations and was immediately followed by the *Favourite* at 1000 tons burthen the largest ship in the port. Twenty thousand spectators roared their approval as cannon were fired from the ships and the battery whilst a "feu de joie" was provided by the muskets of the Royal Invalids belonging to the garrison, and the Nottinghamshire militia. The great merchants then breakfasted aboard the *Manchester* and at noon about three hundred of the principal gentlemen and inhabitants were given a sumptuous entertainment at the Guildhall.

It is disappointing how little notice is given in contemporary sources to the trade in whale products and their commercial use. Typically it is the whale hunt with its aura of adventure and excitement which attracted public attention.

13

Sir Samuel Standidge (1725-1803) one of the founding fathers of the Hull whaling trade. Born at Bridlington Quay he established himself in the North American trade before investing in a fleet of whaleships. A master mariner he sailed to the Greenland fishery on more than one occasion. Mayor in 1795 and five times warden of Hull Trinity House.

Hadley in his history of Hull, 1788, gives a contemporary account of the whale hunt as follows:

"When a whale is seen or heard, a long boat with six men in it (there being always five or six boats ready) makes up to it and endeavours to approach its side near the head; the whale finding itself pursued dives, but rising again to breathe, which it is obliged to do, the men watch the opportunity, row up to its side, and the harpooner strikes him usually near the fin with the harpoon (a triangular barbed iron, about a foot long, and fastened to a stem) the fish no sooner feels the smart, than it darts down into the deep with the harpoon sticking in it; to the harpoon is fastened a line twenty yards long, and as thick as one's finger, which runs with such rapidity after the whale, that if entangled, it must either snap short, or overset the boat; it is therefore one man's business to attend this line, and wet the place on the boat's edge on which it runs, least (*sic*) it should take fire. The boat with the line follows the whale as far as it can, and if the fish be not mortally wounded, he will flounce about in the water for an hour, and draw a line of four hundred yards after him, in which case fresh line is added by other boats. If the fish comes up again alive, they strike it with fresh harpoons, and then kill it with lances; when dead it rises with its belly upwards; should it retreat under the ice, they either pull away the harpoon, or cut the line, in which case they lose the fish, a loss amounting to five hundred pounds, that being its average value. The whale being dead, the first business is to go with a boat into its jaws and cut out the whalebone; they next cut off the blubber from the tongue, and then proceed to strip the whole body of its fat, beginning at the head and tail at once and ending in the middle; forty or fifty men stand on the fish for this purpose, and will finish it in four hours; with the loss of its fat the fish loses its bouyant faculty and when turned adrift, it sinks directly; in a few days it bursts and rises again, and its vast quantity of flesh, affords a large feast to the fishes, birds and bears."

*The Old Dock (Queens Dock) looking eastwards. On the far left is the whaleship **Molly**; she and the neighbouring vessel are furnished with the characteristic crossbeams from which the whaleboats were suspended. This view was engraved and published by Francis Jukes in 1786 from the original study by Robert Thew of Patrington.*

This outline description is inaccurate in a number of details. The harpoon is in fact some two and a half feet long and mounted on a six or seven feet pole of ash or hickory. Attached to it the whale line was given a turn round a bollard, a short, upright, cylinder of wood fixed in the bow of the whaleboat. This took the strain as the whale tried to escape and helped to check the headlong dash which was its usual response when struck with a harpoon. After lancing and killing the carcass was towed back to the ship and lashed firmly alongside. The *total* complement of men was about fifty and not more than three or four perhaps would stand on the greasy surface busying themselves with their knives and spades. Freshly sharpened implements were periodically handed to them by the apprentices occupying a couple of whaleboats along side the dead whale. These craft were referred to as 'mallemauk boats' after the crowds of mallemauks or fulmars which usually gathered round whilst flensing was in progress. Slips of blubber were hoisted aboard using the 'speck tackles', blocks suspended from the 'blubber

15

William Henry Mitchinson master of the **Blenheim** in 1798. He was acquitted of the murder of two naval ratings who died of wounds received while trying to climb aboard and press members of his crew. Mitchinson was latterly master of the **John, Dwina** and **Marquis of Huntly**.

Nᵒ 1191

Port of *Hull*

THESE are to certify whom it doth or may concern, that the bearer *Thos. Stokell* — is a seaman, aged *Nineteen* years, is of a *brown* complexion, *five* feet *eight* inches high, wears *his own dark brown hair loose has a scar on the forehead* — was born at *Hull* in the county of *Hull* and resides at *Hull* in the county of *same town* — that he has been employed *three* voyages in the Greenland and Davis's Straits Trade, and is now entered as a *Boatsteerer* for the ship *Three Brothers* of *Hull* whereof *Josiah Madison* is master, and is to be employed in that ship in the said Fishery, the next ensuing season; and the said *Thos. Stokell* — hath given security to the satisfaction of the honourable Commissioners of his Majesty's Customs, that he will proceed in the aforesaid ship accordingly.

And by virtue of an Act of Parliament, passed in the twenty-sixth, and further continued by an Act in the thirty-seventh, thirty-eighth, thirty-ninth, and fortieth years of his present Majesty's reign, intituled, "An Act for the further support and management "of the Fisheries carried on in the Greenland Seas and Davis's "Straits;" the said *Thos. Stokell* on producing this Certificate, is not to be impressed from or out of any coaster or collier, nor from the said ship *Three Brothers* from the date hereof to the voyage being ended. Given under our hands and seals the *eighth* Day of *March* One thousand eight hundred and *fifteen*

Protection against impressment issued 8 March, 1814, to Thomas Stokell, boatsteerer, of the **Three Brothers** under Capt. Madison. She was lost two years later but all the crew were saved.

*Contemporary model of the **Brunswick**, active in the fishery 1814-34. Note the 'blubber guy', stretched between the fore and main masts, with four large blocks, the 'speck tackles', used for hoisting up the slips of blubber. Note also the particularly heavy stays stretching from the level of the lower yard of the foremast to the bowsprit, and from the main to the stem; the latter divides on either side of the fore mast.*

guy' a stout rope stretched between the fore and main masts. The sixty or more tons of flesh and bone was slowly turned by means of the 'Kent purchase' a massive block hung from the main mast fastened by means of a toggle to a large slip of blubber. Application of a windlass caused the latter to peel slowly, so turning the body and progressively bringing the entire surface under the

flensers' knives. When all the blubber and whalebone had been removed, a process taking three or four hours, the remains were cast adrift for the polar bears and Greenland sharks to eat.

Arriving back in port the cargo of raw blubber and whalebone was taken up to the Greenland yards for processing. The stench of the putrefying blubber several months old can only be imagined, before it was finally rendered down into oil at the boilery. William Etty RA, the noted figure painter from York, was apprenticed to Mr. Peck a printer (publisher of the *Hull Packet*) in Scale Lane between 1798 and 1805 and he sums up the town of Hull as being memorable for 'mud and train oil'. His elder brother Thomas was a seaman in the whaling trade although the ships he served on are not recorded.

Etty's remarks are echoed by William Grimston in a letter to his father dated 27 August 1800:-

"It appears that ths town is never far from annoyance, for the hot weather and whale blubber being over, we have now dirty streets and the smell of the sugar houses to succeed them which I think is if anything worse".

Sailing in Arctic waters contending with the ice and the sudden changes in weather was always dangerous work and Hadley gives us details of the short sad career of the *Whalefisher*:

"In 1785 this unfortunate ship departed from this port on the whale-fishery. On the 30th of April, she stove in both her bows; with much difficulty she was got into the lee pack of ice, and all hands went to work to clear the fore hold of the water, and lumber, which lay forwards, to lighten her by the head as much as possible; the carpenters then began upon the leaks, which they accomplished in about eight hours; during the performance of this repair, they were beset with ice, and were in that dismal situation twenty-one days. On the twenty-second of May they warped out; and on the fourth of June, took a fish of ten feet bone. On the

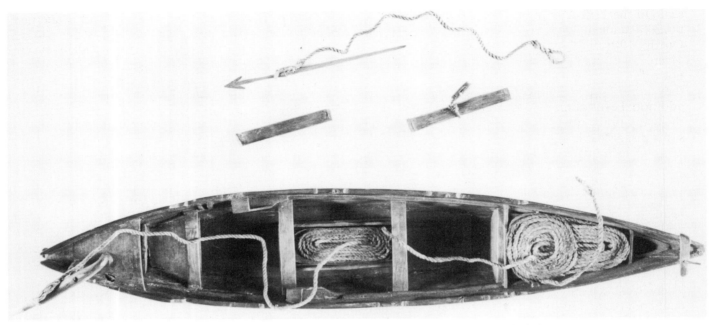

Nineteenth century model of a whaleboat showing arrangement of whale lines
neatly coiled in two compartments by the line-manager.
In this instance the line is spliced to the foreganger of a gun harpoon.
Note hand harpoon with foreganger rope alongside. Two thwarts have been removed for clarity.

eighth they got the vessel off, and cruised among the ice, but met with a very heavy gale of wind, on which they ran into a harbour, called North Bank Bay, in the north latitude 79 degrees 47 minutes, when the captain and the boat's crew went ashore to the Russian huts, where they were informed, that if they would stay the winter, they might get plenty of fish of all sorts, which came into the harbour; the weather was then moderate and fine. On the 4th of June, they came out of the harbour, and on the 8th struck a fish, and lowered all the boats according to custom to kill it, but unfortunately the lines broke, and it got away, and was lost; in hoisting the boats in again, one of the keel bolts drawing out threw one of the men overboard, and the chief mate received a blow of which he died in two days. On the 20th July, they put into a harbour called Cook's Hole, where they buried the mate, and then went out again. On the 29th July they struck a fish, killed her, and some time after arrived in England.

After this narrow escape, the following year in 1786, on the 21st March, the ship was again prepared for another voyage to Greenland. But her very outset seemed to prognosticate an unhappy event, for while the crew were weighing their anchor to go out to sea, they carried away the fore-topsail yard; this accident being remedied by a new one, they got underway, and reached Sunk Island the next day, and put out to sea. On the 11th April they buried a man. On the 20th made the ice, many ships being in sight. On the 10th of May, caught a fish three feet seven inches bone. But this ill-fated ship had not only the natural difficulties of the service they were engaged in to contend with, but the additional evils of internal dissension to render their situation more uncomfortable, there being some disagreeable altercation on board, which was nigh being attended with bad consequences. They then continued cruising for many days in with the land, but meeting with no success, they ran off about twenty leagues steering south south west and struck many whales, but were so unfortunate as to lose them all. On the 3rd June, they got beset with ice, with numbers of fish playing about in holes. On the 18th, they got another fish, ten feet seven inches bone. There were several ships in sight, which they could not reach, but continued in that situation for several days, when they fell in with four sail of Swedes and Danes, with whom they kept company for some time, the weather becoming thick, they lost sight of them all except a Swedish snow; all hands were then employed in sawing docks in the ice, for the safety of the ships; at length it opened in a large hole of water, in which they cruised. On the 29th July, they took a fish of twelve feet bone and then were beset again in the ice for a considerable time; the ice opening they left their comrade the Swede (which could not get out) and descried three sail twelve miles to the north east, which coming up, and the Swedes joining them again, there were then five ships all closely beset with ice. On the 1st of September the *Sally* of London (one of the ships which had joined them) was so blocked up, that a large tongue of ice went through her and all hands were employed in saving the provisions (of which they were in the greatest want) sails, etc. They were divided among the other four ships. On the 9th the ice slacked, and they got under way, and ran about five miles and on the 10th, being in the latitude of 72 degrees, 30 minutes, the ice began to drive at a most terrible rate, and in two hours, they got a heavy crush, and the ship immediately went down being able to save only a butt and a half of bread, and a little beef. The crew were obliged to take to the ice for six days and nights, before the ships would take them in, when they were equally distributed by lot among the other three, to which they were now reduced, two of the five being lost in the ice; amongst which they now remained ten weeks; living on the wet bread, and the Dutch eating theirs dry, as long as it lasted, with the whale-blubber for two months. On the twenty-seventh Captain Allen and thirty of the crew went off in two boats in search of land, and were absent ten days, but were obliged to return for want of provisions, on the 1st of November, when they had the mortification to be refused admittance on board the ships, the Captain offered them bills on London, for blubber to subsist on, which were not accepted; at last they got on board with much difficulty. On the fifth of November, the ice broke up, when they got about seven miles, and were frozen-up again, still subsisting on the blubber. On the twenty-fourth, a gale of wind from the south south east drove the ice, which happily broke up; and on the twenty-seventh, they got safe out into clear water, two ships remained still locked up in the ice till the twenty-ninth. They were forced to keep three pumps going, which took sixteen hands to work, being in want of provisions, they were put to short allowance, having only five spoonfuls of creed barley for breakfast, and two ounces of beef four times a week for dinner, with three pounds of Dutch rusk for nine days, in which situation they remained until the last of December, when they arrived at North Bergen: whence they went on shore for eight days; whence they took their passage to Peterhead in Scotland, then to Aberdeen and soon after by way of Shields, arrived at Hull, having undergone as many hardships in this voyage as any persons (who were not left behind) having experienced, since the whale fishery was first established."

The French wars of 1793-1815 created a need for able-bodied men in large numbers to be recruited for the army and navy. Volunteers were not always forthcoming, especially for the royal navy, so recourse was made to the press gang. Legally a man could be snatched from the streets of his home town or from a British ship at sea and then suffer an indefinite sojourn in the service of the King with the additional disadvantages of harsh discipline and irregular pay. There was seldom even the opportunity to desert which was a frequent resort for the men of the land forces. The press was an institution beloved by no-one including the officers who were given the distasteful job of putting it into practice.

The whaling fleet like the merchant traders sought the protection of the navy from attack by enemy vessels and often travelled in convoy up the North Sea to Orkney and Shetland. They were much less keen to have the attention of the navy on the homeward journey when after a long and arduous season they were eager to get back to their wives and families. In the summer of 1798 the Humber guard ships HMS *Nonsuch* and *Redoubt* fired warning shots in an attempt to halt the whaleship *Blenheim* as she sailed up river. Several boarding parties were fought off with lances and harpoons and Captain Mitchinson locked in his cabin to prevent him interfering. When the *Blenheim* grounded at the entrance of the harbour a Lt. Bell and several companions tried to scramble on deck under cover of musket fire. He and two seamen were wounded in the fight and knocked back into their boat while the whalemen all managed to get ashore and disappear through the crowd which had gathered at the pier to witness these dramatic events. The two navy men, John Burnick and John Sykes, subsequently died and were buried in Drypool Cemetery. Captain Mitchinson was held responsible and tried for murder at the York Assizes but found not guilty and acquitted, the sympathy of the court being entirely with him and his crew.

Crews carried exemption papers, a legal protection against the press though for anyone below the rank of line manager, or not a ship's carpenter, it was valid only from February to the end of the whaling season. Many men were taken despite this supposed immunity but if they were traceable it was sometimes possible to extract a victim from enforced service by the issue of a writ of *habeas-corpus*. An especially outrageous attack took place on the whaleship *Sarah and Elizabeth* when she was boarded off St. Abbs Head, homeward bound, in July 1794. The whalemen fastened themselves below deck and the marines were only just prevented by the master from throwing a grenade into the hold, persuaded of the risk of fire and explosion to both vessels owing to the oil impregnated timbers of the whaleship. Instead a volley of muskets was discharged which killed Edmund Bogg, the carpenter's mate, and wounded three others. Most of the crew of the *Sarah and Elizabeth* were pressed and she arrived in Hull with only fifteen men. Under William Watson Bolton, the coroner and himself a whaleship owner, a jury found that Capt. William Essington of HMS *Aurora* was guilty of wilful murder but to avoid an embarrassing trial the Admiral posted him to the East Indies. He remained at sea for several years, was eventually promoted Admiral and was never brought before a court.

In the early years of the nineteenth century a number of whaling vessels were granted a letter of marque which permitted the installation of cannon. These enabled them to sail independent of the convoys and provide an adequate defence against privateers and warships with their own broadside armament. Some of the South Sea whalers sailing from London with letters of marque seem to have functioned as privateers themselves, actively attacking enemy shipping when the opportunity arose. Papers of the *Caerwent, Cambridge* and *Wilding*, dated 1804-8 specify the vessels of which nation they were permitted to attack and refer to a rendezvous with units of the British Navy in the Atlantic.

CHAPTER 2
THE TOOLS OF THE TRADE.
HAND HARPOONS

The typical hand harpoon was an instrument of iron some three feet long and weighing up to 4lbs. with a barbed head at one end and a socket at the other. A wooden handle of ash or hickory, five or six feet long was inserted in the socket. The pair of flat barbs were wrought on the anvil or latterly were cast from annealed or malleable iron and were soft enough so that the edge could be made with a file. Typically the width of the barbs is not more than six inches and measures six or seven inches along the edge. A small reverse barb, like the beard of a fish hook, was a feature introduced towards the end of the eighteenth century. The reverse barb or 'stop wither' help to fasten the harpoon in the body of the whale by catching on the fibrous connective tissue in the blubber. Previously the harpoon head was a simple arrow shape.

As the vessel approached the whaling grounds the harpoons were sharpened and prepared for use by 'spanning in' (or 'spanning on'). One end of the foreganger rope (2¼ in. circumference and 8-9 yards long) was spliced closely round the shank of the harpoon, the swelling socket preventing the eye of the splice being dragged off. The other end of the foreganger (or foregoer) was spliced to the whale line neatly coiled in the bottom of the boat. There were usually six 120 fathom sections of whale line, a united length of 4320 feet. The stock or handle when pushed into the socket was held merely by friction.

As the prey was pursued in the whaleboat the harpoon lay ready in the 'mik', a wooden crotch on the starboard side of the boat, with the head resting in the bows. If the animal could be approached near enough the harpoon was virtually pushed into its body, otherwise it was lifted to shoulder height and heaved at the target carrying the foreganger rope with it. Once the fish was fast the stock usually shook free. This prevented the otherwise wild oscillations as the whale line tightened and which tended to cause the harpoon to draw. After disengagement the handle remained hanging on the line by means of a cord loop which prevented it floating away and being lost.

A 'fast fish', i.e. a whale with a harpoon stuck firmly in its body, responded by diving deep under water taking out fathoms of line. It was dangerous pursuing a whale through broken ice as the boat might be stove in by contact with any of the more substantial pieces. If the line ran out before the whale surfaced it was common practice for the lines of a companion boat to be bent on whenever possible, otherwise the rope would have to be cut and the chase abandoned.

The shaft of the harpoon was often bent during the efforts of the whale to escape but it was made of good quality iron, soft enough to stretch or distort instead of breaking.

The whale eventually tired and as the boat moved in the crew watched warily for the movement of the enormous flukes. The whale swims by the strong upward and downward beat of the tail controlled by a powerful set of muscles and one strike could smash one of their lightly built craft in pieces.

As soon as they were alongside, the harpooner picked up the whale lance, a spear some six feet long on a four feet wooden shaft. This is the actual killing instrument, the harpoon serves only to fasten a line to the whale to enable it to be played like some giant fish. The lance was repeatedly stabbed into the vital organs until the animal expired and the entire process of the chase, the kill and the tow back to the ship for flensing would take several hours.

There were certain specialist harpoons to hunt the smaller species of whale; the beluga or white whale is particularly soft and yielding and it is difficult to make the harpoon fast. A single-barbed iron was used for

*Harpoon carried aboard the Hull whaleship **Brunswick** which served in the fishery 1814 to 1834 in the ownership of Wright Bowden and Wright. Note the small reverse barbs or 'stop withers', a feature introduced towards the end of the eighteenth century.*

killing walrus, usually attacked on the ice where it was least agile. The harpoon was thrust through the thick hide and twisted so as to catch on the rib cage.

Examination of the head of the harpoon usually reveals the name of the vessel stamped on one side of the shank and the name of the smith and date of manufacture on the other. They were manufactured by a variety of smiths large and small, some local others not. Robert Flinn, blacksmith and whitesmith, of North Shields advertised his harpoons in the Hull press in 1809 and by the evidence of surviving examples the workshop

was active over a considerable period. The earliest belongs to the *Walker* and is stamped 1808 and there are harpoons stamped *Everthorpe* 1828 and *Truelove* 1834. Two others bear the name of John Crosskill, one from the *Ellison* 1828 and the other undated from the *Andrew Marvell*. He was presumably a kinsman of the great Beverley ironfounder William Crosskill. It is intriguing to find the marks of two female smiths though whether they actually wielded the hammer themselves or merely inherited the businesses which bore their name from a husband or father is not clear. The commonest

*Right whale alongside the Scottish whaler **Eclipse** c.1870. Two flensers are poised standing on the carcass of the whale ready to start cutting the blubber.*

identifiable initials A.R. belong to Ann Ross (successor of Aaron Ross) of Castle Street and Railway Street, chain and anchor maker and ships chandler c.1850-60. Another harpoon is signed C. Livingstone for Catherine Livingstone, whitesmith and bell-hanger, of Perrot Street c.1826-35.

Harpoon guns and bomb lances.

The first notice we have of a swivel gun capable of projecting a harpoon is the description of an experiment at Rotherhithe in 1731. Forty years later Abraham Staghold designed an improved harpoon gun which he demonstrated before members of the Society of Arts, again at Rotherhithe, in the Greenland Dock. The gun itself was a typical naval swivel gun mounted on a pivot and with an iron lever at the rear with which to direct its fire. The improvement was in the nature of the missile rather than the gun itself and he established the form of harpoon which was to be universally used thereafter. A foreganger rope, attached to the whale line, was spliced to a ring which travelled freely along the length of the slotted harpoon shaft. Previously the rope had been fastened to the middle of the harpooon so that the weight of the line tended to drag it down out of its intended trajectory, thus reducing both range and accuracy. Staghold, a blacksmith of Stratford, East London, was awarded 20 guineas by the Society of Arts which body ordered six guns and twenty-four harpoons at a cost of 60 guineas which were put aboard two whaleships for the 1772 season. Following a favourable report by their captains, the inventor received a further £30. Humphrey Foord, master of the Hull whaleship *Manchester*, received a series of premiums from 1774 to 1779 for employing this harpoon gun in the Greenland fishery.

These early pieces were not very reliable largely because the lock was too small and hence weak and liable to break. In addition the priming powder was easily wetted by being exposed to the elements rendering the gun inoperable. The successful development of a better weapon was largely hindered by the conservatism of the harpooners, most of whom preferred their hand-thrown weapon to any new-fangled harpoon gun.

Charles Moore, gunmaker of East Smithfield, made a considerable advance in 1790 by enclosing the flint-lock mechanism within the stock of the gun protected by a sliding cover and, for this improvement, he was awarded 10 guineas by the Society of Arts. The gun was primed and cocked, then the cover closed and as soon as the target was in range the harpooner pulled a rod, connected to the trigger, which projected through the butt.

The ultimate development of the flint-lock harpoon gun was achieved in the workshop of George Wallis Jnr.

(d.1833, aged 63) an outstanding Hull gunsmith. In his design, two large flint-locks were placed one on either side of the breech, housed under hinged covers to protect them from wind and spray. By pulling a lanyard tied to the end of the trigger lever directly behind the breech, and threaded through a hole in the wooden stock, the two locks were fired simultaneously to ensure the rapid and efficient ignition of the main charge. An example of the Wallis gun was delivered to William Scoresby, the Whitby whaling captain, in 1813, at a price of 25 guineas with six harpoons costing an additional 9 guineas. It is described and illustrated in Scoresby's *Account of the Arctic Regions*, published in 1820. A chopping knife for blubber, also stamped with the Wallis name probably indicates that the workshop manufactured or retailed the full range of flensing knives and whale lances as well as guns and harpoons. A blunderbuss pistol made by George Wallis Snr. actually utilised one of the main products of the whaling trade by having a ram rod made from baleen (whalebone). George Wallis Jnr. had a family connection with the fishery through his nephew, Richard Wallis Humphreys, master of the *Isabella*, who may well have been involved with the trials of the harpoon gun.

The experiments of the Rev. Alexander Forsyth with various fulminating compounds led to the construction of a wide variety of percussion locks which eventually replaced flint ignition for firearms. William Greener, a Newcastle gunmaker, introduced a gun with a single percussion lock, mounted directly behind the bore of the barrel, protected by a hinged brass cover. A lanyard released a single large hammer to strike percussion caps on *two* nipples placed side by side to prevent misfires. In 1844 the success of his harpoon gun and of his extensive trade in sporting weapons caused Greener to move to Birmingham where his production could expand in the heart of Britain's gun-making industry. The Greener gun became the standard type and this or faithful copies were still being carried by the Scottish whaling and sealing fleet until the outbreak of the 1914-18 War and also by the last of the old sailing whalers operating from the east coast of America

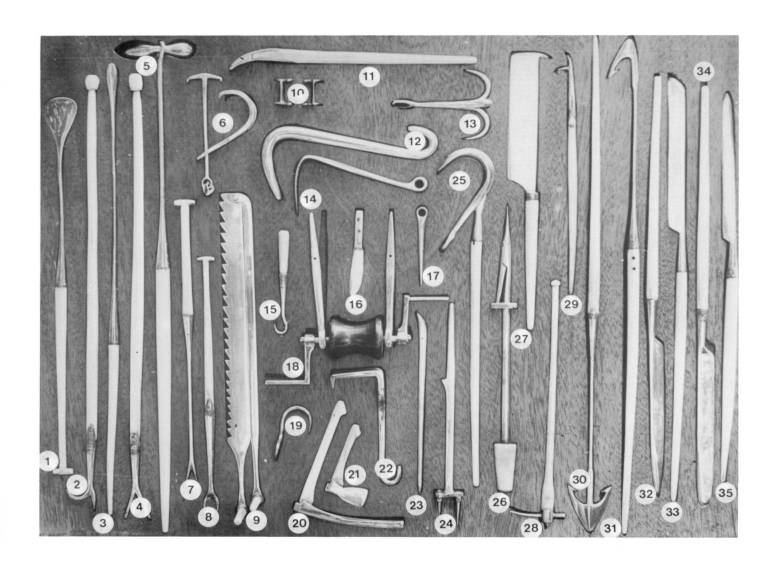

Opposite:

*Set of miniature whaling tools made for the Hull Mechanics Institute which was founded in 1825. (See Wm. Scoresby **An Account of the Arctic Regions, Vol. 2**).*

1. **Blubber spade;** *used to work along the carcass and cut the long strips of blubber.*
2. **Boat hook;** *or long-handled pick-haak.*
3. **Lance;** *spear to penetrate vital organs of the whale.*
4. **Kings fork;** *for pushing the blubber from one place to another; operative who uses it is called a 'King'.*
5. **Gorger;** *apparently to dilate the throat whilst tongue is removed.*
6. **Bone gear;** *four of these with two of the 'speck tackles' on the 'blubber guy' can lift up the whalebone in one mass.*
7. & 8. **Prickers;** *used to push the pieces of prepared blubber through the bung holes of the casks.*
9. **Ice Saw;** *with moveable back, for sawing ice; to create ice docks etc.*
10. **Pair of spurs;** *spiked plates worn on feet to prevent flenser slipping from the carcass.*
11. **Bone hand spike;** *for dislodging whalebone from the skull.*
12. **Ice anchor;** *for anchoring vessel to icefloe or iceberg.*
13. **Grapnel;** *part of the whaleboat's equipment to retrieve lines etc.*
14. **Bay ice anchor;** *for use in thin ice.*
15. **Krenging hook;** *used by 'Krengers' to hold pieces of blubber, thrown from the 'flens gut', whilst any fibrous portions are removed with the **Krenging Knife** (16).*
17. **Marline spike;** *for use in splicing rope etc.*
18. **Boats winch;** *for heaving in the lines after the whale is either killed or has made its escape.*
19. **Hand hook;** *using a pair of these or a pick haak a piece of blubber is mounted on the 'closh'. Also used for generally handling pieces of blubber.*
20. **Ice Axe;** *to chip a hole in the ice to receive the ice anchor.*
21. **Axe;** *placed in the whaleboat in easy reach of the harpooner who can cut the harpoon line if necessary.*
22. **Ice grapnel;** *used in 'warping', it is fastened in the ice front of the ship at the end of a line and the vessel is then hauled through a 'lead' in the ice by taking up the slack of the rope on a capstan.*
23. **Bone wedge;** *to divide head of whalebone into manageable 'junks'.*
24. **Closh;** *set in the deck with spikes uppermost it holds a piece of blubber while the skin is sliced from it with a strand knife or blubber knife by the harpooners.*
25. **Blubber hook;** *for manhandling large pieces of blubber about the deck.*
26. *Instrument of uncertain use.*
27. **Chopping knife;** *to cut the blubber into pieces small enough to ram through the bung holes of the cask. Also to cut off skin when on the closh.*
28 **Seal Club;** *the seal could be stunned by a blow on the nose and killed with the spike driven into the back of the skull.*
29. **Pick haak;** *like a short-handled boat hook, used for passing portable pieces of blubber through the hatches to the 'Kings' who pack it in the 'flens gut' awaiting further treatment.*
30. **Hand Harpoon;** *characteristic British type, twin barbed with small reverse barbs or 'stop withers'.*
31. **Hand Harpoon;** *single barbed (for walrus?).*
32. **Tail Knife;** *for perforating the fins or tail of a dead whale ready for towing.*
33. & 34. **Blubber Knives;** *used along with the spade for stripping blubber from carcass i.e. for flensing.*
35. **Strand Knife;** *to divide the large strips of blubber removed from the carcass into manageable pieces for temporary storage in the 'flens gut'.*

A 'spur' one of a pair of spiked plates worn on the feet when standing on the carcass of the whale during flensing.

bomb lance, a metal cylinder filled with gunpowder which was shot from the barrel of a conventional harpoon gun in place of the harpoon. Principally it was intended for speeding up the kill and dispensing with the bloody and laborious work with hand lances which were churned inside the vitals of the whale until it expired. It might also be used to try to capture species not normally within the capabilities of the Arctic whalers, like an attempt in 1859, which failed, to kill a blue whale recorded by William Barron in his memoirs.

"As we were pulling close to the floe which was six feet above the water edge, a large finner rose close to us. I drew the harpoon and wad out of the gun and replaced them with a bomb lance. These lances were of very recent date, and had only been in use about a year. Not having tried one before, I thought this a good opportunity to prove the efficiency of them. The finner, which was above one hundred feet long, was only fifty feet from us, and formed a barrier between us and the outside. I did not think of our position, being too intent in trying what effect the bomb lance would produce. We were so well situated that I could choose to strike it any part of the body, so took aim behind the left fin and fired. I then perceived our critical position. If it had rolled towards us instead of from us we should have been crushed, as there were no means of escaping on the ice. Immediately the bomb entered the body the animal appeared paralysed, and in a few seconds the bomb exploded, and we felt the vibration. Then the body appeared to expand, and rolled from us in agony, giving a great flourish with its fins and tail, causing the water to nearly fill the boat, and wetting us to the skin. The next we saw of her was about a mile away. blowing blood and swimming at a rapid rate through the water."

down to the 1920's. The very last was the Bark *Wanderer* which made her final voyage in 1924 at a time when the modern whale factory ship had already made its debut.

In 1859 a Hull gunsmith named Edmund Balchin registered a patent for the 'Construction of a Projectile applicable to the whale fishery'. This was a variety of

Edmund Balchin (1825-88);
photographed in 1879 when he was
master of the Humber Lodge of Freemasons.

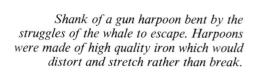

Shank of a gun harpoon bent by the
struggles of the whale to escape. Harpoons
were made of high quality iron which would
distort and stretch rather than break.

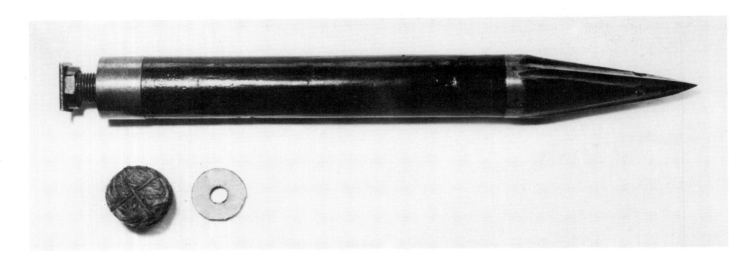

Balchin's bomb lance before insertion of match at rear.

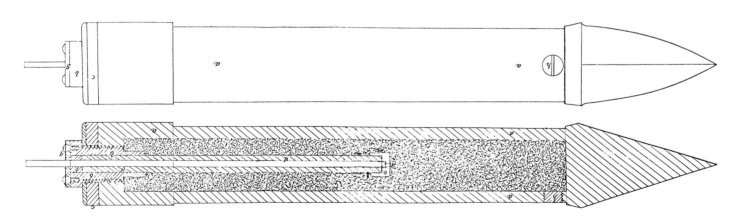

Diagramatic section of Balchin's bomb lance.

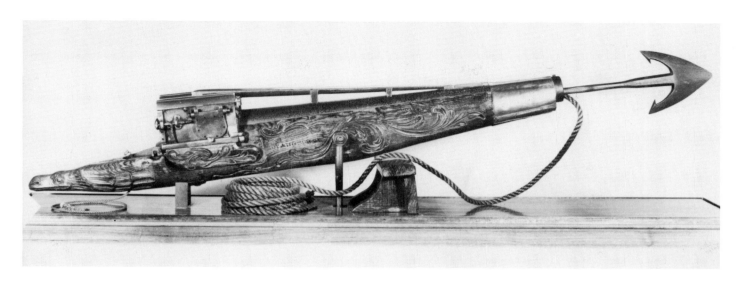

Flintlock harpoon gun by George Wallis of Hull.
*Used on board the **Royal George** active in the fleet 1805-21.*
The butt is handsomely carved into the form of an eagle's head.

This trial was made from one of the whaleboats of the brig *Anne* and it is interestiong to note that Balchin owned five shares in the Whale and Seal Fishery Co. owners of this vessel from 1860 until her loss the following year. He also maintained an interest in the Hull Fishing Co. which took over its assets in 1866.

A tube containing a fuse match inserted at the rear of the lance was ignited when the main charge went off. Extending some distance to the rear of the cylindrical missile, the fuse was vulnerable to damage. Barron goes on to say:

> "Great precaution must be used with them, the powder in the gun must not be pressed too tight, or the fuse is liable to bend, and in consequence it will not ignite. Another time one exploded in the muzzle of the gun, and rent the barrel down to the breech like a piece of paper!"

Despite these hazards the bomb lance was invaluable when a whale already fastened with a harpoon attempted to escape under the ice. A lance fired into its vital organs would stop it dead in its tracks.

31

CHAPTER 3
THE EARLY NINETEENTH CENTURY

The typical whaling ship of the late eighteenth and early nineteenth centuries was a full-rigged ship, occasionally a bark, with a burden of some 300-350 tons. Vessels left Hull in the spring with a full complement of some fifty men and stopped off at Lerwick to take on fresh provisions and fill up the water casks. The latter were carefully arranged to ensure a stable trim and provided ballast until the whaling started and blubber began to accumulate in the hold. More and more vessels sailed to the Davis Strait and in the early nineteenth century Hull gained an unchallenged presence in the Arctic fishery. At the peak of its development in 1819, soon after the end of the Napoleonic Wars, sixty-five vessels left the port, the majority for the Davis Strait. At first they penetrated only as far as Disko (70°N) and Jacob's Bight (71°) but soon began pushing further north.

This route pushing up to the head of Baffin Bay and across the clear North Water to the Canadian coast had been charted by the *Larkins* and *Elizabeth* in 1817. This route was firmly established when three years later the *Cumbrian, Early Fauconberg, Friendship, Ariel, Truelove* and *Duckenfield Hall* followed the same path.

It was the voyage of Sir John Ross in 1818 in search of the North West passage which confirmed the existence of the North Water, a large area of open water at the northern end of Baffin Bay. If ships reached here, having negotiated the treacherous Melville Bay on the north Greenland coast, they could then work across and down the west side of Davis Strait. A virgin territory, until then only known to the Eskimo, the numerous bays were endowed with an abundant population of Greenland whales.

The exploitation of these new grounds was essential because of the declining stocks in the traditional Greenland fishery off Spitsbergen and east Greenland. It meant however that the actual voyage to the fishery was considerably lengthened and in these far northern waters beyond the Arctic circle the fleet was more vulnerable than ever to the vagaries of the northern climate. Melville Bay in particular became a notorious graveyard for ships. Here heavy ice and contrary winds often hindered progress, seriously reducing fishing time. Vessels would not infrequently become trapped, beset and finally crushed in the ice.

During the French wars when so many men had been swept up by the army and navy it was increasingly difficult to make up a crew. It became the custom therefore to leave home port with a basic sailing crew, harpooners, and specalists such as a cooper, carpenter and blacksmith. There were enough men to handle the ship and keep watch but the rest of the complement was made up by the doughty island men of Shetland and Orkney. Inured from an early age to handling small boats in their sea-girt homes their strength and dexterity in pulling an oar provided the motive power for the pursuit of the whale. The Orkney men were taken aboard at Stromness by the Davis Strait vessels and the Shetland men at Lerwick when bound for the Greenland fishery.

In the early nineteenth century not more than fifteen or so island men would be taken aboard, often much less, but in the 1850s and 1860s when the fleet was greatly reduced, as many as half the total crew might be recruited in the north. These were usually Shetland men since a sealing stint at Greenland usually preceded a voyage to the Straits. While they were being mustered and provisions and water taken aboard there was time for the remainder of the crew to enjoy a trip ashore, the only landfall before embarking for the Arctic seas. A graphic description of one of the Lerwick drinking dens is given by Christopher Thomson, carpenter's mate on the *Duncombe* in 1820:-

The **Lord Gambier** of Kirkcaldy, the only known photograph of one of the old sailing whalers. Built at Monkwearmouth she was originally in the Newcastle fleet but transferred to Hull in 1845. After eight seasons the **Lord Gambier** was sold to Kirkcaldy making her last voyage to the fishery in 1862.

Barrel crow's nest of the type devised by William Scoresby Snr. in 1807. Slung from the top of the main mast on chains it was entered from the bottom by a trap door. A canvas hood could be rotated to give shelter from the wind. The occupant was provided with a telescope for observation along with a signal flag and speaking trumpet to communicate with the crew below.

33

"One of my shipmates, who was to initiate me into the revelries of the island, took me to a whiskey shop. On my entering it, I was really afraid; never before had I seen such a stew, into which were huddled such a number of human beings. The place was one dense pit of smoke. In these cabins there were no chimneys: the fire, which is usually made of peat, smoulders away upon the mud floor in the ingle; the smoke pervades the whole area, and then lazily makes its escape from the door. The roof and walls of these "smithies" are as black as a moonless midnight in December. As I stood a few paces within this pitchy den, I trembled; my eyes were smarting with the effects of the turfy fire. Around the glimmer, in the ingle, were seated a troop of crones, attired in course grey woolsey petticoats; over their heads were thrown a dark plaid, just showing their brown profiles; some of them were knitting; each had a short black pipe, blowing away their "bacca" and chattering in broad Gaelic. This shop was literally stowed with both sexes, the greater part of them sailors, some singing, others swearing coarse oaths. In the centre of the den, two of the tars were reeling with a dark-eyed island girl, to the drone of a bagpipe, driven by an old and lank-jawed piper, attired in a grey serge jacket, and leaning against the smutty wall. Here was such a commingling of the low and ridiculous as I had never before witnessed — a strange looking lot, dimly visible through the veil of peat-smoke, singing, roaring, and stamping their feet to the mysterious "naw-a-aw-a" of the piper. I knew of no parallel to it. It was like the entrance to the fabled pit of Acheron, and here were the infernals assembled, to yell over their hellish mysteries; yet the sailors called it a fine pastime, and drained their pockets, and mortgaged the voyage to prolong it!"

Though the whaling trade was a hard one which involved a constant battle with the polar climate there were times even at sea when the men could enjoy some good raucous fun. May-day was celebrated by hoisting the garland on the main top-gallant stay, a good luck token usually in the form of a circlet or wreath surrounding or surmounted by the silhouette of a ship. The task of tying it to the main top gallant stay was the prerogative of the most recently married member of the crew. All novices, referred to as "greenhands", entering the Arctic for the first time were then duly initiated by King Neptune, a ceremony paralleling that still performed when crossing the equator:

"May-day morning was made a rejoicing with the English ships in this land of eternal hoar and ice, and called the "Greenland Fair". As soon as midnight is turned, and blithe May begins her reign, the Greenlanders hoist the garland. This garland is a contribution of ribbons from every man and boy on board; a Greenland sailor would as soon think of going to sea without his pea-jacket, as to go without his garland ribbon! Before leaving home, the sweethearts of the single men usually present their beaus with a garland ribbon, and generally they present it at their farewell meeting, so that they are love-tokens. Upon each ribbon, the charmer ties as many knots as she wishes her lover's ship to bring home fish. Anciently the lover was not permitted to count these knots until May-eve; if he told them before the hallowed night, the spell was broken, and the knots were of no avail. The married men often procure their garland ribbons from persons who are considered fortunate in this world of chances — as the blind god, "Fortune", it is expected will kindly extend his assistance to this knotty matter of the garland!

May morning is the time when the young voyager is to be admitted to the full honours of a true Jack Tar; his probationary duties are to

The **Harmony (I)** owned by Robert Bell and then by his son Thomas
is seen anchored by the bow hawser to the neighbouring ice floe.
Note the May Day garland hanging from the main top gallant stay.
This picture is derived from the original by W. J. Huggins painted in 1829.
It was also engraved by Edward Duncan the artist's son-in-law and the print dedicated to Thomas Bell.

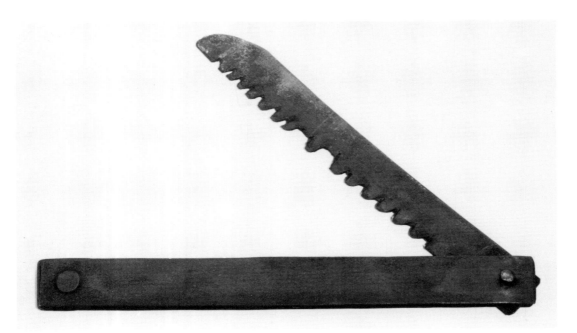

Joke razor, made from the hoop iron of a barrel, used in the May Day ceremonies when King Neptune initiated the Arctic 'green-hands'.

cease at the express command of Neptune himself, who directs him to be *shaven* according to his own heart. The novice has to make certain oblations of rum, coffee, sugar, or such agreeables he can best spare! These Neptune generously gives up for the good of the crew. Upon the liberality of the probationist in the giving department depends in great measure, his comfort during the shave. This May-day shaving in the North, is twin-brother to the ceremony of shaving practised upon those who "cross the line" in warmer latitudes. The approach of Neptune is made known by a loud stamping of the crew upon the deck, and amongst other requisites, he takes care to put on a tremendous long beard, made of horse hair; he is also decorated with a mimic trident, and mounted upon a gun carriage: The made-up sea-god is now mounted on the forecastle, and the novices are there summoned to his presence! He expresses his joy at seeing them, and assures them of his great condescension in personally welcoming them to the seas of Greenland. He is then drawn around the deck, laying first the captain under contribution, then descending to the secondaries. During the triumphal progress of the tobacco-mouthed Ocean-king, the garland is hoisted, and it usually remains until the vessel reaches home.

When his godship is enthroned below deck, his myrmidons commence the ceremony of shaving. A large tub is provided, filled with water, across it a plank is placed (the barber's chair) upon which the luckless wight is seated to be shaved. Around his neck is twisted a wet swab — this swab made of a great number of small yarns, tied together, and about four feet long, it is used for drying the decks after washing. This appendage is kindly ordered by the King, to keep the lather out of your neck. Then follows the lathering with a compound of tar and other offensive ingredients. During this part of the ceremony, the prime operator is flourishing about for his razor, a large piece of iron hoop, set in a coarse wooden handle, and notched on the edge like a saw. When the shaving is about to commence the noviciate is asked "what he is going to present to Neptune, as a remembrancer of his visit?" If the present be considered sufficient then you "could not be sooner shaved in a barber's shop" — but if it be a stingy one, then, poor fellow, he may expect the lather to be profusely applied — the plank drawn off the tub, and a cold duck into it to wash off the lather; and to be used rather roughly into bargain.

My propitiation was a bottle of contraband whiskey, bought at Lerwick for that purpose, according to my father's direction, whom experience had well schooled in these matters."

There was constant hazard navigating amongst the broken pack and the vessel was conned through the ice by a lookout at the main top mast. Until about 1807 when William Scoresby Snr. the Whitby whaling captain, invented the crows nest, the watcher was protected only by a scrap of canvas as he guided the ship through the narrow "leads" which opened and closed with changes in the wind and current. The crows nest was a large barrel, suspended from the mast with chains, providing protection from the biting Arctic winds for the occupant seated inside scanning the surrounds with his telescope. Whales could be spotted many miles away as they came up to the surface to recharge their lungs. A great double spout of water droplets became apparent as the warm stale air rapidly cooled in the atmosphere. If the quarry was close enough and there was clear water between ship and whale a boat would be launched to start the chase.

Sometimes a boat might be dragged a short distance over intervening pack ice and a successful strike was followed by a general mobilisation. Up to seven whaleboats could be used each with six or seven men so that the mother ship was often left with only a handful of men to mind her:

"The Greenland sailors always sleep in their drawers and stockings, and have their remaining clothes tied together with a "gasket", and hung up conveniently, near to their bed-cabin door, to allow of them being caught hold of in an instant. As soon as the strange shout of 'A fall' is heard, every man is expected to jump up, seize his bundle of clothes, and rush on deck, and into the boats, which are immediately lowered away, and pulled, with all the energy the men can summon, towards the boat which has already "got fast", or in other words, the one which has first harpooned the fish. As soon as the boats are under weigh, the crew put on their clothes by turns — putting on one article of dress, and then pulling until your mate has put on one also, and so on whilst all are dressed; the crew have often to go for several miles before that is completed."

After flensing and 'making off', i.e. chopping and packing the blubber into barrels, the off-duty whaler might find a little time for recreation, playing cribbage with his shipmates or just lying in his bunk enjoying a pipe of tobacco. The more enterprising would whittle or carve pieces of bone or baleen and decorate them in a variety of ways.

Unlike the South Sea whalers with their voyages lasting two or three years there was relatively little spare time.

When not on watch or involved in the whale hunt or its aftermath the crew was likely to be busy sawing ice docks or 'warping' the vessel through the pack either when there was no wind or it was dangerous to hoist any amount of sail because it was blowing too hard. A Davis

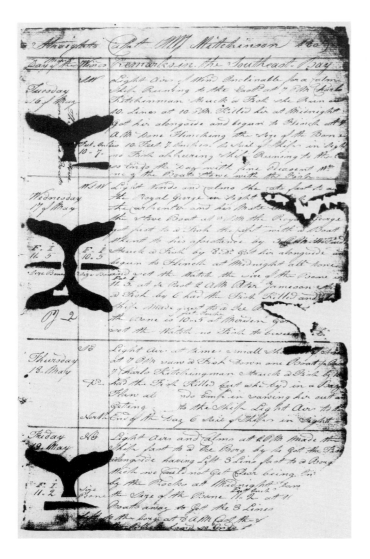

*Page from the log of the **Marquis of Huntly** of 1809 her only voyage to the fishery. She was lost the same year apparently while trading, and in the sole ownership of John Barmby of Sutton. Her commander, Capt. Mitchinson achieved notoriety at the time of the **Blenheim** affray in 1798. Each kill is marked by a whale's tail and the length of the longest piece of 'bone' in each animal is also recorded. The lower example is 11ft 2in which implies a large whale: the maximum was not more than 15 feet.*

moved to Hull in 1819 where his daughter Sarah had settled with her husband John Skelton. Both Sarah and his wife died that year and on 13 September at Holy Trinity church he married Hannah Seaton. His ship the *Fame* sailed from Hull for the first time in 1820 and was eventually re-registered in this port in 1823, in which year Scoresby was resident at 50 George Street. The vessel was destroyed by fire while at an anchor in Orkney that year and this signalled the end of Scoresby's sailing career. He retired to Whitby where sadly his last years were marred by a coolness between himself and his son. Aged 60 and in a state of derangement he shot himself, a tragic end to a brilliant career.

Though there had always been losses it was in 1821 at the height of Hull's commitment to the fishery that the first truly disastrous season was experienced. From a total of sixty-one ships, nine were lost though happily the crews were saved. The solitary representative from Grimsby, the *Earl Fauconberg* was also lost as were the *James* of Newcastle, the *Dexterity* and *Larkins* of Leith and the *Elizabeth* of Aberdeen. The shock of these losses resulted in a reduction of the fleet by a third to forty vessels in 1822 and from then until the end of the Hull fishery the highest number ever to leave the port was forty-one — the year after that. Despite the risks the emphasis on Davis Strait continued so that in 1830 the whole of the fleet of thirty-three ships was fishing on the west side of Greenland. As it turned out this season was to be another serious setback for the northern whalers and six vessels were lost and a further eight returned without having caught a single whale. Hull did however

Strait voyage was typically eight months from March till October and a 'full ship' might return from the Greenland fishery in July or August.

William Scoresby Snr. of Whitby, one of the outstanding whaling masters of the nineteenth century,

A CORRECT STATEMENT

OF THE

Success of the Hull Ships at the Greenland and Davis' Straits Fisheries,

In the Year 1821.

GREENLAND. ·—·◄·—·▬▬·—·►·—· **DAVIS' STRAITS.**

Ships' Names.	Register Tonnage. (tons pts.)	No. of Men.	Captains' Names.	Date of arrival at Hull	No. of Fish.	Actual weight of Fins or Whale Bone. (tons. cwt. qr. lb.)	Actual quantity of Oil boiled. (tuns. qr. gall.)
North Briton	262 ,,	41	John Allen	Aug. 2	10	6 16 0 7	167 3 29
Perseverance	251 ,,	47	Matthew Wilburne	— 10	10	8 6 3 13	151 1 9
Everthorpe	349 ,,	47	Robert Ash	— 16	11	9 19 1 12	182 1 30
Cicero	325 5	41	William Leaf	— 21	7	4 13 2 1	101 1 47
Mercury	316 25	48	William Jackson	— 21	13	7 14 3 20	16) 3 44
Elizabeth	321 ,,	45	Thomas Rhoades	— 22	10	5 16 2 20	15) 0 36
Truelove	293 70	43	Thomas Todd	— 23	3	2 17 1 7	54 2 6
Walker	335 ,,	49	Richard Harrison	— 25	7	5 14 0 26	105 0 24
Laurel	321 ,,	41	Edvard Dannatt	— 25	7	4 5 1 7	95 0 34
Manchester	285 ,,	46	John Mitchinson	— 25	5	5 16 1 0	30 2 59
Shannon	348 ,,	41	Robert Kelah	— 25	4	2 11 3 26	5 3 33
Ebor	283 23	49	Thomas Lee	— 26	5	4 8 0 11	8 3 35
Venerable	328 ,,	41	John Bennet	— 27	10	4 17 0 17	11: 0 4
William Torr	280 80	46	Phillip Dannat	— 27	5	3 2 0 16	61 2 57
Dordon	285 90	49	William Gilyott	— 27	4	2 14 1 5	5) 0 22
Neptune	336 17	49	Martin Munroe	— 30	5	4 2 1 3	7.. 3 60
Alfred	303 ,,	49	William Clark	— 30		Clean.	
Gardiner and Joseph	360 ,,	41	James Angus	— 31	7	2 19 3 19	84) 1 38
Exmouth	321 41	41	Edward Thompson	— 31	1	2 2 18	5 0 24
Cyrus	346 48	42	William Beadling	— 31	7	4 9 1 22	9 0 11
Mary and Elizabeth	317 27	34	Robert Williams	Sept. 1	4	6 2 11	2 51
Abram	319 14	48	William Harrison	— 1	8	2 13 0 8	51 0 55
Trafalgar	330 ,,	46	William Lloyd	— 1	7	4 3 1 3	98 3 41
Duncombe	270 ,,	45	John Corbett	— 13	9	6 3 3 2	136 3 4
Eagle	289 ,,	49	William Brewis	— 13	14	7 13 1 3	15, 0 58
Harmony	300 ,,	43	Charles Sawyer	— 13	3	2 10 2 27	5? 2 24
Fame	377 12	56	William Scoresby	— 19	9	6 12 3 22	112 3 15
Jane	359 ,,	41	Stephen Gamblin	— 20	1	1 8 3 9	1? 2 37
Cato	305 ,,	41	Andrew Turnbull	— 20	1	No Bone.	5 1 46
Unity	272 81	35	William Short	— 22	11	5 18 3 21	117 2 54
Rachel and Ann	223 84	40	Richard Marshall	— 25	14	7 0 3 23	144 3 28
Total. 31 Ships	**9665 33**	**1376**			**204**	**135 10 3 15**	**2745 2 7**
Average each Ship	311 73⁵¹⁄₃₁	44⁴¹⁄₃₁			6⁶⁄₃₁	4 7 1 2²⁶⁄₃₁	88 2 16⁵¹⁄₃₁

Ships' Names.	Register Tonnage. (tons pts.)	No. of Men.	Captains' Names.	Date of arrival at Hull	No. of Fish.	Actual weight of Fins or Whale Bone. (tons. cwt. qr. lb.)	Actual quantity of Oil boiled. (tuns. qr. gall.)
Ellison	357 61	47	John Johnson	Sept.19	13	10 15 0 15	170 3 56
Cumbrian	375 34	55	John Johnson	Oct. 4	28	12 14 1 25	213 3 34
Zephyr	342 ,,	41	John Unthank	— 6	19	14 0 0 0	213 2 52
Gilder	360 7	41	George Bruce	— 6	19	12 19 0 23	219 0 33
Brunswick	357 ,,	52	William Blyth	— 7	24	14 15 3 12	269 0 30
Andrew Marvel	377 ,,	41	Thomas Orton	— 13	18	13 1 1 15	215 2 61
Albion	321 61	48	Richard Humphreys	— 17	21	12 15 1 7	214 1 39
Kirk Ella	410 72	49	Henry Watson	— 17	6	5 1 3 13	80 1 57
William	350 ,,	46	Thomas Hawkins	— 17	12	7 15 3 10	129 1 47
Lee	363 ,,	41	Thomas Forster	— 17	11	8 14 2 20	123 2 4
Kiero	358 ,,	46	James Colquhoun	— 17	4	3 10 3 20	53 1 24
Egginton	336 27	47	John Wilson	— 17	8	6 17 2 4	114 2 17
Lord Wellington	354 ,,	41	John Boydon	— 18	15	10 4 3 26	144 1 52
Progress	307 56	49	Matthew Mercer	— 18	8	5 5 3 16	97 2 57
Mary Frances	3*5 73	41	Thomas Wilkinson	— 18	14	8 4 2 6	161 0 21
Ingria	316 ,,	49	James Mackintosh	— 19	29	1? 8 1 1?	28d 1 53
Royal George	368 28	49	Joseph Peckit	— 20	9	5 9 1 19	108 0 0
Friendship	410 ,,	49	George Green	— 21	6	4 1 2 21	80 0 15
Ariel	340 ,,	49	William Hurst	— 21	12	6 7 0 15	118 0 23
Thomas	355 ,,	41	William Brass	Nov. 6	10	7 10 1 7	128 3 1
Margaret	349 22	41	James Creighton	— 6	8	4 4 2 6	76 2 46
Total. 21 Ships	**7482 55**	**963**			**294**	**186 19 1 12**	**3142 3 6**
Average each Ship	356 29⁵¹⁄₂₁	45⁹⁄₂₁			14	8 18 0 7⁹⁄₂₁	149 2 39⁴⁵⁄₂₁

GRAND TOTAL AND AVERAGE FOR GREENLAND AND DAVIS' STRAITS.

Total. 52 Ships	**17147 88**	**2339**			**498**	**322 10 0 27**	**5888 1 13**
Average each Ship	329 72⁸⁴⁄₅₂	44⁵¹⁄₅₂			9⁴²⁄₅₂	6 4 0 4²⁵⁄₅₂	113 0 59⁴²⁄₅₂

☞ The Refuse, or Black Oil, is not included in this Account, nor the number of Men taken from Shetland and the Orkneys.—The John, 343 Tons; Symmetry, 342 Tons; Harmony, 378 Tons; Leviathan, 409 Tons; Henry, 314 Tons; Cervantes, 355 Tons; Aurora, 368 Tons, Lost at Davis' Straits, Crews saved.—Thornton, 262 Tons, Lost at Greenland.—Hebe, 364 Tons, Lost on her passage to Davis' Straits, Crews saved.

AGGREGATE STATEMENT OF THE NUMBER OF THE HULL SHIPS FROM THE GREENLAND AND DAVIS' STRAITS FISHERIES, FROM THE YEAR 1772, WITH THE QUANTITY OF OIL, &c.

Year.	No. of Ships.	Tuns of Oil.		Year.	No. of Ships.	Tuns of Oil.		Year.	No. of Ships.	Tuns of Oil.		Year.	No. of Ships.	Tuns of Oil.		Year.	No. of Ships.	Tuns of Oil.	
1772	9	391		1782	3	217		1792	20	896	3 Clean	1802	34	2955		1812	49	6812	1 Captured
3	9	265	2 Clean	3	4	290		3	18	835	1 Clean	3	41	2262	2 Clean	3	54	3533	3 Clean
4	8	466	1 Lost	4	9	432		4	16	709	1 Lost	4	40	4018	3 Lost	4	57	7379	1 Lost
5	10	6*8	6 Clean and 2 Lost	5	15	722	1 Clean	5	14	1148	1 Clean	5	38	5165	1 Lost and 1 Captured	5	55	3607	3 Clean, 1 Lost
6	9	275	1 Lost	6	19	856	1 Clean and 1 Lost	6	17	1578	1 Captured	6	39	3524	3 Captured	6	55	5150	1 Lost
7	9	333		7	29	1132	1 Lost	7	21	1741	1 Lost	7	35	4350	2 Lost	7	57	4789	1 Clean, 1 Lost, 1 Broken up
8	8	171	2 Clean	8	34	958	3 Clean	8	23	2162		8	27	4556	3 Lost and 2 Captured	8	63	6219	1 Lost
9	3	142	1 Lost	9	27	854	2 Clean and 2 Lost	9	26	2244	2 Lost	9	26	4321	3 Lost	9	60	5077	3 Lost, 2 Broken up
1780	4	309		1790	23	832	2 Clean and 1 Lost	1800	22	1818		1810	41	5019		1820	60	7978	2 Lost, 1 Broken up
1	3	263		1	18	345	4 Clean and 3 Lost	1	24	2149	1 Lost	1	42	5398	1 Lost,	1	52	5888	1 Clean, 9 Lost

☞ The lost and captured Ships are not included in this number of Ships.

Hull: Printed by T. Topping.—Sold by W. Dawson, 47, Lowgate.

1821 was the first really disastrous season for the Hull fleet when 9 vessels were lost. Of the 52 vessels which returned 31 had visited Greenland and 21 Davis Strait. A total of 2339 men sailed as crew from Hull in these fifty-two ships, an average of nearly 46 each which implies an average of 4 men taken on board at Orkney and Shetland. This would still make some 200 islanders. Over all 494 whales were caught producing 322 tons of whalebone and 5888 tons of oil, more than half from Davis Strait. Of the survivors only the **Alfred** *returned clean. Note the signature and address of Robert Morley Sawyer, son of Charles Sawyer of the* **Harmony**.

remain the major British whaling port and in 1835 again sent out twenty-three ships; her nearest rival was Peterhead with eleven, followed by Kirkcaldy, seven, and Aberdeen, five; all of course in Scotland. The once significant whaling contribution from Whitby was reduced to two and London only one.

The 1835 season proved another great hammer blow to hopes of recovering the declining fortunes of the fishery with the loss of another five Hull vessels and only two of the returning vessels carried the produce of more than two whales.

Back in the peak years catches were usually in double figures, averaging ten per ship and individual catches might exceptionally be more than thirty 'fish'.

On the 4th December the Hull shipowners sent an address to the Admiralty apprising them that eleven vessels had been left behind in Davis Strait owing to the early onset of winter conditions. They had insufficient provisions to enable them to overwinter with any confidence of survival and there were on board these ships over six hundred men, including the survivors of three vessels lost the previous year.

The Admiralty agreed to commission a ship, pay the crew and furnish stores, if the shipowners and underwriters would fit her out and man her with volunteers. Additional funds were raised by public subscription, two of the organising committee were George Ross, brother of Sir John Ross, and Sir Felix Booth, who had financed the latter's 1829 expedition. James Clark Ross (nephew of Sir John) was appointed as commander and Richard Wallis Humphreys, the experienced Hull whaling captain, was his ice-master. Humphreys supervised the preparation of the Hull whaleship *Cove* and two hundred men worked day and night so that within a fortnight she was ready for sea. Ross departed from Hull 6 January 1836 and made great progress until they encountered a violent storm which took away the bowsprit and damaged some of the interior beams. Forced to return to Stromness for repairs further delays caused by contrary winds delayed the

departure of the *Cove* until 24 February. In the meantime, the *Jane* and *Viewforth* arrived with the survivors of the *Middleton* on board. Fourteen men of the *Viewforth* had been victims of scurvy and another thirty or so were seriously ill, with only seven capable of work. Ross leased an empty house as a temporary hospital for the stricken men before sailing north once again. News had also arrived of the command of the *Abram* with nearly one hundred men aboard and only the *Lady Jane* and *William Torr* were still unaccounted for. A whaleship outward bound gave Ross news of the return of the *Lady Jane* and he continued north as far as the islands searching for the sole missing whaler. He encountered nearly fifty vessels of the new season's fleet detained by ice near Disko Island and after sailing across to the Labrador coast, decided to head for home after gaining no reliable news of the *William Torr*. The *Cove* arrived back in Hull on 31 August and it was eventually discovered that the *William Torr* had been crushed in the ice in December 1835.

The next year was also a failure and though there were no actual losses eight of the fifteen ships returned 'clean' and the remainder caught a combined total of fourteen whales. As a reaction to these events eight of the eleven entrants in the 1837 season departed for the old grounds on the east side of Greenland hoping to enhance their catch by pursuing seals as well as whales. A total of something over two thousand seals were procured and eighteen whales and from Davis Strait two vessels returned 'clean' and only the *Duncombe*, Capt. Dean, made a reasonable catch and brought back the produce of four whales amounting to 58 tons of oil. On the 2nd July the *Swan* returned to Hull after being beset the previous season and given up for lost. From 1838 to 1842 the fleet declined from six to a mere two, the *Jane* and the old faithful *Truelove* which had originally entered the fishery in 1784. Peterhead was now the leading port with ten ships and out of the total British fleet (in 1842) of eighteen, fifteen sailed from Scotland and Newcastle sent only the *Lady Jane*.

This nadir marks the end of the first and greatest phase of Hull whaling and though the trade was to continue for nearly thirty years more it never again reached its former heights. Between 1754 and 1842 one hundred and eighty-six Hull vessels participated in the Greenland and Davis Strait fisheries. Of these, six were captured by the French, and sixty-six were lost plus another three after transfer to another port, a 40% loss of what were usually well found, full-rigged ships of not less than 250 tons burden.

CHAPTER 4
WHALEBONE, OIL AND SCRIMSHAW

The mouth of the right whale has some three hundred horny plates on either side of the mouth. Each is a more or less elongated triangle in shape with the inside edge frayed into a hairy fringe. The fibres of the adjoining sheets of baleen are tangled together to form a sieve by which the whale extracts its food from the sea water. Each mouthful of water is squeezed through the baleen as the tongue is distended leaving behind a mass of small planktonic organisms which are the staple diet of the 'whalebone whales'. Whalebone is the vernacular word for this material but it is entirely different from skeletal bone (which is comprised of calcium phosphate) and is a ceratinous substance akin to horn. An immensely useful and versatile material it is durable and flexible and can be cut, sawn or moulded. We hear of it being used in the Middle Ages to make the decorative crests of tournament helmets and even the blades of the mock swords used in 'jousts of peace'.

Baleen was also a major component in the composite crossbows of the fifteenth century replacing the horn found in many examples. A rare pressed baleen panel of Dutch origin depicting a "Bacchanalian frolic" (dated c.1618-41) is in the Kendall Whaling Museum, Sharon, Mass.

Most often it is recorded as a stiffening element in various parts of the elaborate court dress worn both by men and women. Many yards of 'whalebone' formed the farthingale, a framework which stretched out the skirts of the ladies of the late sixteenth and early seventeenth centuries. These creations might be four feet or more in width as can be seen in some of the paintings of Queen Elizabeth and in the court portraits of the Spanish artist Velazquez (1599-1660). The fluctuations of fashion always had a significant impact on the price of 'whalebone' which was in considerable demand in the early eighteenth century for the contemporary hooped petticoats. Even in 1766-69 it was fetching £398 a ton, but this was to fall to £102 in 1795 largely because of the increased supply from a much expanded whaling fleet. Umbrella ribs were another staple use until Samuel Fox of Sheffield began to supply his umbrella steel in 1852. In 1808 Samuel Crackles of Hull patented a method of cutting plates of whalebone so as to provide an effective substitute for brush bristles. The patent passed to John Crackles, 'Patent Brush Manufacturer' of Silver Street who successfully defended its infringement at the York Assizes. Furthermore he and his partner offered a twenty guinea reward to anyone who gave information regarding any contraventions by rival makers. John Bateman and Robert Bowman of Silver Street were active at the same time and advertised a tremendous variety of whalebone goods. These included sieves, nets, ornamental blinds, bed bottoms, stuffing for upholstery and brushes. Sir John Sinclair in an address to the Board of Agriculture, 7 June 1808, recommended whalebone nets, another of their products, for confining sheep, "as much more durable, and in other respects greatly to be preferred, to any article of the same sort and in use".

The lightness and resilience of baleen was recognised by Thomas Walker the Hull portrait painter and author of *A Treatise Upon the Art of Flying by Mechanical Means* (1810):

> "I think that the shafts of the wings and tail would answer the purpose in the best manner, if they were each of them made of six long slips of thin whalebone, dressed tapering to a point, then wrapped together in a round form with small twine, from end to end; and filled with cork along the inside. By making them in this manner, they would spring against the air, would be very light, and so strong, that it would be impossible to break them with the power or weight of any one person".

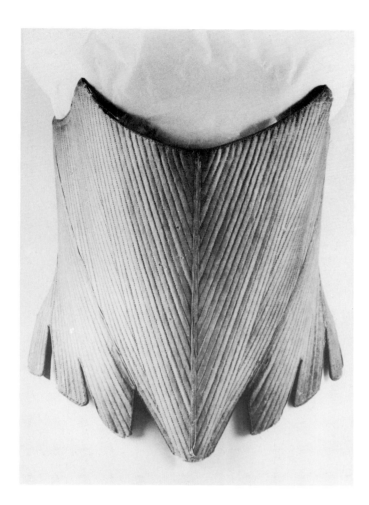

Early nineteenth century stays. No less than 160 narrow strips of whalebone (baleen) are stitched between two layers of canvas. These garments were much more flexible than their counterparts at the end of the century.

Separating the plates of whalebone (baleen) using a flensing spade while resting on a chunk of blubber as a chopping block.

Frame of a shed made from pairs of Right Whale jawbones.
It stood in the Esk Valley near Whitby and was dismantled in 1930.

The whalebone was cut from the gum before separating the individual blades with the aid of a blubber knife. As far as possible the fleshy residues were removed before sending the bundles of baleen down into the hold. When the cargo was discharged at the Greenland yards for sorting and processing the plates were thoroughly scraped and cleaned. Beckett and Wake in 1812 advertised a new machine for this very purpose "by which considerable labour, time and expense, will be saved". It was claimed to be small enough and cheap enough for each Greenland owner to install one on his own premises and employ his own labourers.

Towards the end of the Hull whale fishery the price of whalebone was about £500 a ton which meant that even though the price of oil was depressed a profitable voyage could be made when only two or three whales were caught.

By 1885 the elaborate Victorian corset and an increasingly restricted supply of raw material pushed the price up to £1500 a ton. In 1902 when the apogee of feminity was the hour glass figure of the Gibson girl whalebone was £3000 ton. The unhealthy and body deforming fashion was however being achieved mainly with the use of steel rather than baleen, the supply of which had almost dried up.

The whale jawbones themselves were put to use and were often bought by local farmers and gentry to set up on gateposts referred to as "jaw-bone yat-steeads" in East Yorkshire dialect.

The only jawbone arch surviving within the present city boundaries intact and in its original location is to be found in the grounds of the Elms, Lowgate, Sutton. This land was originally part of the estate of the Bell family, oil merchants and owners of the whaler *Harmony*. On 15th June 1991 on behalf of the Sutton in Holderness Society the present author unveiled a plaque adjacent to the whalebone arch, commemorating Thomas Bell, owner of the *Harmony*.

A receipt dated 21 September 1820 of Charles Sawyer,

the master, records nine pairs of jawbones being brought home with a value of £14.3s.6d.

Three pairs of jawbones still stand in the garden of what used to be the Fisheries Museum at Pickering Park on the Hessle road. Two of these are from the framework of a canvas-covered whalebone shed which stood in the Esk valley at Whitby and was taken down in 1930. The third pair was removed from Kirkella. A jawbone brought to Hull in 1820 by the *Andrew Marvell* was presented by a Mr. Stanton, one of the crew involved in the capture of the whale, to Dr. Beale Cooper in his home town of Evesham, Worcs. The arch was transferred in 1906 from the doctor's estate to the Workman gardens alongside the river Avon where it can still be seen.

For the homeward journey from the Arctic they were usually tied wishbone fashion to the mast so that any oil draining from the jaws could be collected. Once the whaleship arrived in port the 'whalebone', jawbone and barrels of blubber were transferred to lighters and taken up the river Hull to the Greenland yards, situated on the east bank mostly in the Groves and Wilmington area. Jawbones and sometimes flipper bones were rendered into bone meal for improving the land. Any residues, the "fenks", from boiling out the blubber, along with scraps of whalebone and tail ends were pressed into a compost for manure. The tendinous fibres of the tail might be utilised for glue-making and any fibrous material left over from dressing the whalebone would be collected for stuffing upholstery.

Whale oil was used as lamp fuel, the preparation of leather and coarse woollen cloth and as the basis of varnishes and paints. A useful lubricant for machinery it was also in the days of sail mixed with tar for application to ships cordage as a general preservative to prevent it rotting and becoming waterlogged. Early in the nineteenth century coal gas began to compete with it for street lighting and illuminating the grander houses and mansions but this in turn encouraged the production of a gas from whale oil itself. This burned with a much

Whalebone scrapers in the Greenland yards of Whitby or Hull.
This illustration was originally published in George Walker's **Costumes of Yorkshire***, 1814.*

THE
WHALEBONE
MANUFACTORY,
South street, Kingston-upon-Hull

G. R.

By the King's Letters Patent.

The Public is respectfully informed, that Orders are received and executed with the greatest punctuality and dispatch, for

*SIEVES and RIDDLES of every description.

NETS, with Mashes of various Sizes, for folding Sheep, preventing Hares and Rabbits from passing through Enclosures or Pleasure Grounds, or entering young Plantations.

SLAYS, for Weavers.

TRELICES or GUARDS for Shop-windows, Gratings for Granary, Barn, Warehouse, or Cellar Windows.

Ornamental BLINDS, for House Windows, of various Patterns.

CLOTH of great durability for the preservation of Meat, in Larders, or Safes.

BED BOTTOMS, in place of Sacking.

CARRIAGE BACKS and SIDES; CHAIR and SOFA BACKS, and BOTTOMS, in Black, White, or other Colours, after the manner of Cane in any Pattern.

STUFFING, for Chair and Sofa Bottoms and Backs at a lower Price, and preferable to Curled Hair.

BRUSHES, of different sorts. With a variety of other ARTICLES.

John Bateman,
AND
Robert Bowman.

* Extract from the last address to the Board of Agriculture, by Sir John Sinclair, Bart. on the 7th. June, 1808.—"The "Whalebone Sieves, and Nets for confining Sheep, invented by Mr. Bowman, are evidently much more durable, and in "other respects greatly to be preferred, to any article of the same sort now in use. It is certainly desirable also, by increas- "ing the consumption of Whalebone, to promote our fisheries, which, like other branches of domestic industry, cannot be "too much encouraged."

MYRTON HAMILTON, PRINTER, SILVER STREET, HULL.

Hand bill advertising the products of
Bateman and Bowman's Whalebone Manufactory,
South Street, Hull, in 1808.

brighter and cleaner flame than its rival but this was only a temporary reprieve and it could not compete with the much lower prices of coal gas made on an increasingly large scale. Whale oil lost ground to colza (rape) oil in domestic lamps and finally to paraffin after mineral oil (petroleum) began to be extracted from the North American wells.

Colza oil was also better for the treatment of the higher quality cloths and so there was an inevitable conflict between the interests of the whale oil merchants and the textile manufacturers. The duty of £21 a ton on imported rape oil imposed in 1809 was lifted in 1825 and the lobby of whaleship owners and Hull members of Parliament had to admit defeat.

The seals which became more important as the century progressed were a source of a high quality oil. Their skins had a limited use in the fashion trade to make into coats, hats and purses. They also provided a hard-wearing and decorative cover for trunks and chests.

Portions of baleen or whale jawbone were cut and decorated by the whalers in their spare time. Bone plaques and bone cribbage boards are known, but the most popular item seems to have been the stay busk. A piece of baleen some fourteen inches long and two inches wide it was a present for the whaleman's wife or sweetheart who inserted it in the front of her bodice and wore it literally next to her heart! A unique description of the preparation of such items comes again from the pen of Christopher Thomson, carpenter's mate aboard the *Duncombe* in 1820:-

"I was often employed in what the sailors dignified by the title of 'bone carving', which art consisted in cutting on the bone, with a penknife, diverse cyphers of the initials of their sweethearts, with borders of diamonds, squares and vandykes, or "tooth ornaments"; the interstices were filled up with chalk and oil, which brought out the pattern; as in addition to the given round of ornaments, I could add panels

Whalebone (baleen) stay busk 16¾in long; 2in wide) decorated with simple geometric designs and ships scratched in the surface. It bears the initials BG – SH and inscribed in ink is the doggerel verse:

'Sailors they are bound for
all weather, great winds blow high
or blow low Our duty keeps us
to our teather (sic) and
w(h)ere the wind blow we do to (o)'

of whales, ships, birds and "Prince of Wales" feathers, the latter was a stock ornament at that period; besides if it had not been so, what tar in 1820, could be so loyal as to forget thePrince Regent, afterwards George the Fourth, of "pious memory?" For these ornate decorations I received sundry mess-pots of grog."

Walrus tusk was also available as a raw material providing a kind of ivory prepared in the same way as the sperm whale teeth of the South Sea whalers. The surface was polished with sharkskin and the design scratched into the surface. A mixture of lamp black and oil provided a pigment which filled the lines engraved with a penknife or sail needle and made an excellent contrast to the white ivory. Quantities of walrus tusk were also still being brought into Europe for decorative carving, mainly the handles of umbrellas, parasols and walking sticks. They were also made into false teeth though porcelain replaced this natural material and the modern dental technician uses various kinds of plastic. The value of walrus greatly diminished as plentiful supplies of elephant ivory began to arrive at the port of London from our African colonies.

The tusk of the narwhal had been one of the great treasures of the middle ages when it was regarded as being the horn of the fabulous unicorn. Huge sums of money were paid for them by the Kings and Princes of Europe and powdered 'unicorn horn' was regarded as an antidote to poison. Even when its true origins became more widely known it was an essential constituent of cabinets of curiosities and the early museums. Whalers still called narwhals "unicorns" ('unies' for short) even in the nineteenth century and found a limited market for these extraordinary appendages. Narwhal tusks are in fact true ivory and derive from a massive development of one of the upper incisors. They are characterised by a spiral growth and can in extreme cases measure some nine feet in length. A pair in the Town Docks Museum, Hull each mounted on a wooden block, formed two of the supports of a canopied bed. Shorter examples were sometimes used by gentlemen as a very elegant form of walking stick. As a rule the ivory was not decorated but the spiral pattern might be enhanced by carving and then given a highly polished finish.

It is now usual to refer to as *scrimshaw* all the items made and decorated by the whalemen themselves from

A Unicorn's horn (narwhal tusk) preserved as a curiosity at Parham Park, Sussex. First documented in 1561 it stands some 80in in a lockable case carved and painted to resemble an Elizabethan jousting lance.

*Samuel Cooper, whaleship owner, born in 1775 at Nottingham, a principal owner along with his brother William S. Cooper (1783-84) of eleven vessels including the **Samuels, Brothers, William** and **Swan**.*

bone, ivory and baleen. The men of the English whaling fleets had no particular name for their sparetime activity which was just part of the tradition of whittling and carving common to all seamen throughout the merchant and royal navies. Scrimshaw derives from the English dialect word 'scrimption' meaning a very small piece, a miserable pittance. It was first used in its restricted and specific sense by the Yankee whalers in reference to the scraps and unwanted pieces of whalebone and ivory which were doled out at the discretion of the master and his officers.

CHAPTER 5
WHALESHIP OWNERS

The ownership of each vessel was divided into sixty-four shares and as a general rule there were two or three principal owners and perhaps three or four subsidiary shareholders not directly involved in the management of the vessel. It was unusual for a vessel to be entirely in the hands of one individual and the *Unity* was exceptional in having as many as ten 'non-subscribers' in addition to the principals, mostly small shopkeepers and artisans but also including a Pocklington surgeon and a gentleman of Hessle.

Almost half of the chief shareholders described themselves as merchants and nearly a quarter were mariners which is explained by the fact that the master usually held a share in the ship he commanded and maybe other vessels as well. Of the remainder some are merely listed as ship owners without further indication of status or occupation and there are thirteen gentlemen, three bankers, a banker's clerk and a merchant's clerk. The roll-call includes five shipbuilders, as well as ropemakers, a ship chandler, ship broker and an insurance broker, all representing maritime-related activities. There is also a cabinet maker, a wheelwright and a cooper and the latter may well have had a commercial interest in whaling since barrels were an essential part of the ship's stores for the storage of blubber. Shareholders further include a farmer, a corn factor, a hosier, four woollen drapers and one auctioneer. A victualler, grocer and butcher may all have been in the business of supplying the whaling fleet with provisions. The tally is completed with one spirit dealer and two brewers.

Hull's biggest whaleship owners were Gardiner and Joseph Egginton, oil merchants and seed crushers. Their father came to Hull from Nottingham and these two brothers were twins born on 21 June 1761, Gardiner being the eldest. Between 1804 and 1833 they were principals in no less than fourteen whaleships and were lucky enough to lose only four of them. Joseph was Chairman of the Hull whaleship owners from 1813-25 which was very much the heyday of the local fleet. He had also been sheriff of Hull in 1793 and mayor in 1798 and 1804 as well as deputy lieutenant of East Yorkshire. Joseph died on 15 December 1830 aged 67 and was buried at St. Andrew's parish church (close to his home at Kirkella House) where there is a fine gothic memorial. Gardiner Egginton lived at Aston Hall, N. Ferriby.

Samuel Cooper and William Spyvee Cooper follow a close second to the Eggintons, with a controlling interest in eleven ships. Their father also came from Nottingham and the two brothers ran the family ropery in Lime Street which no doubt supplied the cordage for their whalers. A large oil painting, the grandest of all pictures of the Hull whaling fleet, executed by Robert Willoughby in 1803, was evidently commissioned by the Coopers and shows five of their vessels, the *Thomas, Brothers, Samuels* and *North Briton*.

Samuel's son, Dr. Henry Cooper, was an eminent figure in Victorian Hull. Physician to the infirmary and later active on its board of management, he served two terms as mayor. On the first occasion in 1854 he was knighted by Queen Victoria during her visit to the city with Prince Albert during which the latter officially opened the Royal Institution. In honour of the occasion, the "old dock" and the Junction Dock were renamed the Queens Dock and Princes Dock respectively. The Coopers were actively involved in the whaling trade from 1805 to 1838, but they were less lucky than the Eggintons and seven of their vessels were lost in the Arctic.

John Marshall, only ever described as a shipowner, had a major interest in twelve ships, four of them with Samuel Cooper, between 1805 and 1826; only three were lost in service. William Watson Bolton, another of the whaling moguls, was surgeon to the Hull General Infirmary, but resigned in 1798 to devote himself to

*Built at Plymouth in 1767 the ship **Swan** was originally a naval gun brig which accounts for her fine lines.*
Sold out of the service after involvement in the Nore mutiny she was acquired for the whale fishery by Samuel Cooper in 1815.
After thirteen seasons in the Arctic she was broken up in 1840.
The model maker has suspended a miniature whale from the 'Kent purchase' hung from the main mast.
It is entirely out of scale and this tackle was in fact fastened to a large slip of blubber
to progressively bring the entire surface of the whale under the flensers' knives.

STOLEN,

FROM the Greenland Ship LORD WELLINGTON, Captain LAMBERT, lying in the Old Harbour, near to Mr.GIBSON's Ship Yard, on FRIDAY Night last, about

20 *Fathoms of Warp,*

AND SUNDRY OTHER ROPES:

FROM the Greenland Ship PERSEVERANCE, WILLIAM NESBITT, Master, also lying in the Old Harbour, opposite Messrs. KNOX SHAW & Co's Quay, on FRIDAY Night last,

About 8 Fathoms of a Tackle-fall,

And, 4 or 5 *Fathoms of a 4-Inch Warp:*

And, on SUNDAY Night last,

The Remainder of the Warp,

(ABOUT 12 FATHOMS)

Which had been left, after the Depredations committed on Friday Night.

ON BOARD the Greenland Ship SHANNON, Capt. KEILAH, and several other Greenland Ships, various Depredations have been committed; and sundry Parcels of ROPE and CORDAGE have been STOLEN.

Whoever will give information of the Offender or Offenders, so that he or they may be brought to Justice, shall receive a Reward of

Five Guineas

On a Conviction for each Theft, committed on board the above-mentioned Ships; to be paid by the Committee of Owners of Greenland Ships belonging the Port of Hull.

By Order,

Martin & Scholefield,

HULL, 26th Dec. 1814.   SOLICITORS.

William Ross, Printer, Bowlalley-Lane, Hull.

Thomas Bell (1786-1851) of Sutton,
*oil merchant and owner of the whaleship **Harmony**.*
The family originated in Northumberland but Robert Bell his
father settled at Hull in the late eighteenth century
as a spermaceti candle manufacturer,
oilman and shipowner. Their memorials can be seen
in Sutton Parish Church.

*Reward offered by the whaleship owners of Hull after the theft of rope and cordage from the **Lord Wellington, Perseverance** and **Shannon** in December 1814. They would have been laid up refitting ready for the following season.*

business as a shipowner, oil miller and underwriter. He was principal in nine craft, eight of them jointly with Christopher Bolton (merchant) who was probably his brother.

The family were closely involved in the municipal life of the city. W. W. Bolton was sheriff in 1792 and mayor on two occasions 1794 and 1802. Christopher was sheriff in 1812 and mayor in 1815 and 1822. One might also note that Christopher was a trustee in the Cogan Charity School along with Joseph Smyth Egginton (son of Joseph Egginton) and Nicholas Sykes. The Boltons lost four of their fleet in the fishery, the *Hunter, Mary and Elizabeth, Symmetery* and *Henry*.

The shipbuilder, William Gibson of Great Union Street, was a major shareholder in seven vessels (three were lost), one jointly with Samuel Cooper and John Marshall, two with Edward Gibson and another with Robert Gibson. He and his sometime partner in shipbuilding William Hey Dikes each held a half share in the *Harmony* (III), while the *Cumbrian* and *Brunswick* were held jointly with Wright, Bowden and Co. Only two of the seven vessels were built on the Humber but neither of these, it seems, at the Gibson shipyard. The *William Lee* was built by Dikes and Gibson, but neither man invested in her. Edward Gibson was sheriff of Hull in 1824 and mayor in 1834.

W. H. Dikes is described as a bank manager in some sources and was a Fellow of the Geological Society. An active supporter of the Hull Literary and Philosophical Society he was appointed as the first curator of its museum in 1823.

The Bowdens who were Russia merchants (i.e. traders with the Baltic), James Allen and Thomas Jackson all made significant investments in the whaling trade. William Lee, tar and turpentine distiller and whale oil merchant, was sole owner of the *Experiment* (I) and the *Lee* and initially the *Nelly* and *Prescot* too, but a portion of their shares passed to Robert Lee. William and Robert were sole owners of the *Thornton*, probably named after Samuel Thornton (1755-88) who was a

director of the Bank of England and in 1784 elected a member of parliament for Hull on a joint ticket with William Wilberforce. His father, John Thornton (1720-90) was first treasurer of the Marine Society and Director of the Russia Co. He married Lucy, daughter and heiress of Henry Watson of Hull, probably a kinsman of J. K. Watson, the banker. James Kiero Watson was a shareholder in the *Mary Frances* and the *Kiero* though the Eggintons were the chief owners of the latter. Henry Thornton, younger brother of Samuel, married the only daughter of Joseph Sykes, iron merchant of West Ella, an eminent Hull merchant. He was a firm supporter of his cousin, William Wilberforce, and the two of them were the founders of the evangelical group known as the Clapham Sect after their regular meeting place at Henry's House, Battersea Rise, on Clapham Common.

A whaleship called the *Clapham* was jointly owned by Jeremiah Wright, James Shrapnell Bowden of Hull, Benjamin Wright of Clapham, Charles Hobhouse of the City of Leeds, and William Rust, a Hull goldsmith. It seems likely that the Wright family and their associates were also active in the Clapham Sect.

The biggest soap manufactory in Hull was established by John Thornton and Benjamin Pead. The latter's memorial stone in Sutton parish church is sited close to those of the Bell family (oil merchants and whaleship owners) and describes him as 'citizen and sope (*sic*) maker of London, but late of this parish, who died the 11 October 1784 aged 54 years'. Whale oil and various vegetable oils were the raw materials for soap-making and after Thomas Lee entered the firm, which became known as Pead and Lee, paint-making became an important side-line. The two men were the founding fathers of the Hull Subscription Library which was formally established in 1775.

Of the lesser shareholders a third are described simply as merchants, gentlemen form the next biggest category, followed by mariners. There are seven bankers, two bankers clerks, two merchants clerks, a commercial

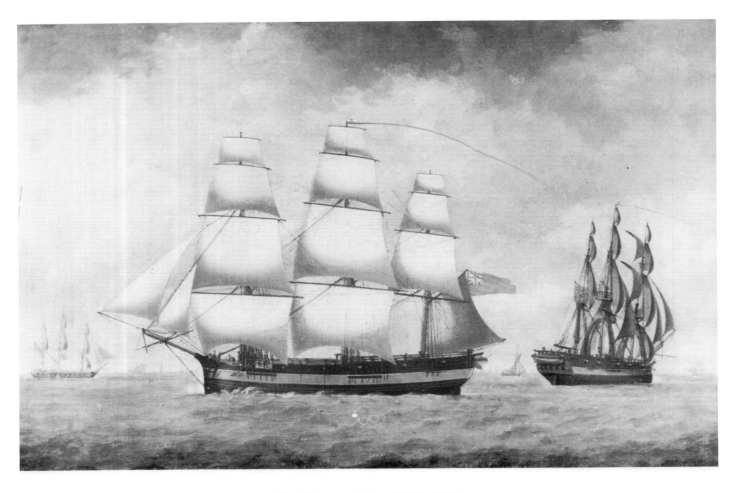

The **Thornton** built at Hull in 1789,
and owned by William Lee. She made her first whaling voyage in 1803 and was lost in 1821.

Whale shoulder blade sign still displayed outside the
'Royal Children' public house at Castle Gate, Nottingham.
Just such a sign would have been shown outside
the Whalebone (or Splawbone) tavern in Wincolmlee.
Its presence in Nottingham seems to be another indication
of the trading contacts between
Hull and the north Midlands through the
Trent navigation system.

agent and a broker. In the maritime trades there are six shipbuilders, four sailmakers, one mast and block-maker, one roper and four timber merchants. Two coopers are also listed as well as an oilman, who was probably an oil processor rather than a merchant. An anchor-smith may also have had a commercial link with the whaling trade since harpoons were often one of the products of the anchor and chainmaker. There are also six linen drapers, a laceman, two wool staplers, a hosier, cloth merchant and flax merchant as well as a number of farmers, two millers, three butchers, one baker, a grocer, sugar refiner, confectioner, victualler, innkeeper, maltster, three brewers, two wine merchants and a spirit merchant. There is also a bricklayer, a cabinet maker, silversmith, earthenware dealer and limeburner. Finally there is a druggist, three surgeons, and four ministers of religion, one a dissenter, the others of the Anglican persuasion.

There was a strong commercial trading link between Nottingham and the Humber; the Trent formed the outlet for Nottingham and for Derby lead which was shipped to Hull by barge for export. As we have seen both the Eggintons and Coopers had Nottingham origins and Abel Smith II, grandson of the founder of the Nottingham bank, founded banks in Hull, Lincoln and the City of London. He was also a partner in the Baltic merchant firm of Wilberforce and Smith. He was related to Wilberforce through his wife Mary Birch whose sister was the mother of the great emancipator.

Gainsborough, which had been an important port on the Trent since the Middle Ages, had a vital role as a link between the Humber, the agricultural region of Lincolnshire and the industrial Midlands. John Newbald of Gainsborough was a subsidiary share-holder in four vessels of the Cooper fleet, the *Samuel, Brothers, North Briton* and *Ingria* between the years 1805 and 1826. He acquired a holding in a fifth vessel, the *Ocean*, from James Hewetson who was also involved in the *Samuel, North Briton* and *Ingria*. A note in the *Hull Advertiser* for 3 February 1832 records that

Bill of Hawkins and Robinson, 58 High Street, Hull, in 1832.
Edward Hawkins was an oil merchant and John Robinson a chemist, druggist,
oil and colourman.

Newbald's house in Chapel Staithe had been burgled while his family were attending chapel, some silver spoons and other valuables were taken.

In 1809 William Bourne a Gainsborough rope-maker was advertising in the *Hull Packet* his patent whale lines which again emphasises the Lincolnshire town's involvement in the fishery during the early nineteenth century.

Two Gainsborough men, William Mercer and John Tidd, oil and seed merchants, were co-partners in the firm of Mercer and Tidd and together owned the *Abram*, 1819-41, *Mary Frances* 1828-36 and *Mercury*, 1820-27. John Sooby, another Gainsborough merchant, was a subsidiary shareholder in the *Mercury* who, with John Stuart, also of Gainsborough, was a 'non-subscriber' in the *Abram*, 1814-21. John Tidd was a subsidiary owner of the *Cherub*, 1817-19 as were William Mercer, John Sooby and John Stuart. Tidd was elected treasurer of the Gainsborough Stock Library in 1836 and in 1840 several lots of property belonging or leased to Tidd and Mercer were put up for auction. These were the Trent Port Mill with its adjacent cottage, wharf and field, the Bridge Oil Mill with its adjoining warehouses and outbuildings as well as Mr. Mercer's house, Mr. Tidd's cottage, a windmill and dispensary. The firm of Tidd and Mercer had broken up and Mr. Sooby, who purchased the Trent Oil Mill, joined in a new partnership with Mr. Mercer.

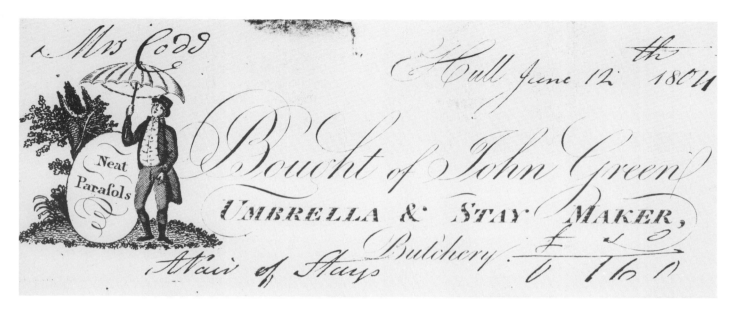

Bill-heading of John Green, umbrella and stay maker of number 14, Butchery, Hull; a pair of stays sold to a Mrs. Codd, in 1804, cost sixteen shillings. He had moved to Queen Street by 1810, and was last recorded at 36 Savile Street in 1823.

Thomas Torr, merchant of Gainsborough, was principal owner of the *Riby Grove*, along with the Hull merchant T. B. Morley, 1818-25, and then with John Torr, merchant of Hull, until the vessel's loss in 1838. His maximum holding was 52 shares but there were transactions with other members of the Torr family, 4 shares to William Torr of Riby (Lincolnshire) in 1833 and 8 shares to Thomas William Torr, a Hull merchant, in the same year. The whale-ship *Riby Grove* was named after the estate near Grimsby occupied by the Tomline family after 1600, and bequeathed by them to George Pretyman Bishop of Lincoln, c.1883. Thomas Torr was the head of Thomas Torr and Co. listed in the Hull trade directory for 1817 as Baltic Merchants, seedsmen, Newcastle crown glass and lead warehouse. T. W. Torr, merchants and shipowners, had their offices at 36 High

Street and in 1848 Thomas William was living at Dairycoates Grange, a large house which vanished with the construction of St. Andrew's Dock and the North Eastern Railway tracks. John Torr lived in one of the fine dwellings which formed Bellevue Terrace on the Humber bank and the firm which bore his name is listed until 1843 at 47 High Street, the same address as Thomas Torr, and variously listed as general merchants, Baltic merchants, commission agents and shipowners. The *William Torr*, lost in 1835, was jointly owned by Thomas Torr and George Rudston, a woollen draper, of Newland.

William Etherington, another Gainsborough merchant, was a small shareholder in the *Richard* (from 1810) and with Joseph Peters Smith of Burton-on-Trent in the *Dordon*, 1820-6. The latter vessel was launched at Gainsborough on 3 February 1820 from the yard of Henry

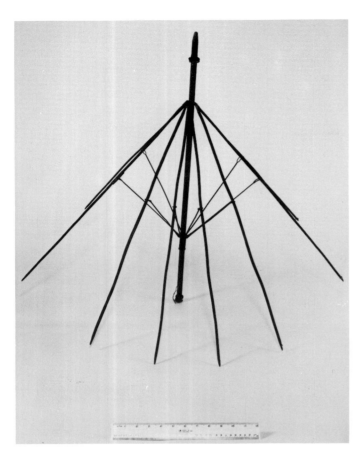

Umbrella with ribs of whalebone (baleen).

Smith who had married Etherington's daughter, Rachel, twelve years previously. Henry Smith, described as a merchant, and John Smith of Hull, were the principal owners, 1820-36, with lesser holdings in the hands of Thomas Cox, merchant, Derby, Elizabeth Hammond, spinster, Hull, and Thomas Freer, gentleman, who resided in the village of Dordon in Warwickshire after which the vessel was named. The whaler *Trafalgar* built at Gainsborough in 1806 in an unnamed yard was owned by William and Christopher Bolton of Hull. Gainsborough's role in shipbuilding has yet to be fully explored but current research shows that Moody's yard launched a paddlesteamer in 1815 and this was probably the first steamer engaged in a regular cargo and passenger carrying role actually built in England. The first such vessel on the Humber was the Scottish-built *Caledonia* which entered service in 1814.

The decline after the disasters of the 1830's was followed by a revival, but in the ensuing quarter of a century the *total* number of vessels involved in the trade was only thirty-eight, which compares with over sixty ships sailing from Hull in a single season during the peak of activity. The character of the vessels becomes heterogeneous and includes small vessels such as brigs and smacks and the principal shareholders were equally mixed. The largest group, about one sixth of the total, describe themselves simply as merchants, another tenth are mariners. In addition there are three gentlemen, three bankers, one banker's clerk and an attorney's clerk. The clothing trade is represented by a bootmaker, hatter, tailor and draper. There is a cabinet maker, optician, pipe maker, silversmith, seed crusher, corn merchant and land agent. Of trades directly concerned with the sea, there is a wharfinger, ship chandler, and shipbuilder. Grocers are well represented and manufacturers and purveyors of food and drink form the biggest grouping, about a fifth of the total, and in addition to the brewers and grocers there is a fishmonger, baker, victualler, provision merchant, and wine merchant. Finally there is a druggist, a colour merchant, a colour manufacturer and a painter. The three latter categories have a connection with the whaling trade inasmuch as whale oil (as well as linseed and vegetable oil) were employed in the mixing of paints. Druggists and apothecaries usually sold sperm oil for medicinal and household purposes, though at this period it would all have been imported from America or our Australian colonies. Seed crushers produced vegetable oil from various imported seeds and often were concerned in the processing and sale of whale oil too. Two of the purchasers Councillor J. T. Robson, were active in the seed-crushing industry. Henry Hodge purchased Blaydes House, High Street c.1850 and built an oil mill close by on the river side.

The lesser shareholders of the period show a similar cross-section with the addition of five shipbuilders, a roper and a mast and block-maker. There is also a builder, ironmonger and a joiner, corn merchant, tallow chandler and a soap merchant. The latter may have included soft soap made from whale oil among his wares. Purveyors of food and drink comprise one sixth of the total, the largest group of related trades and occupations. Along with five drapers, we also find a tailor, a wove-stay maker and horse-hair manufacturer. The two latter may still have been using whalebone for stays and upholstery stuffing as and when it was available.

CHAPTER 6
OF SHIPS AND MEN

The Truelove

The story of the *Truelove* is very much the history of the Hull Whaling trade through its heyday, decline, revival and final demise.

She was built in 1764 on the Delaware at Kensington, Philadelphia, the first large vessel to be built by the brothers Manuel and Jehu Eyre. Employed as a privateer she was captured by a British cruiser during the American War of Independence, brought home as a prize and was purchased in about 1780 by a Hull wine merchant, John Voase. She was first placed in the Oporto trade but in 1784 the *Truelove* made her first Greenland voyage as one of the nine vessels then in the Hull fleet. Sometime prior to 1789 her already sturdy frame was sheathed and doubled and she was lengthened and almost rebuilt in 1790. Surprisingly therefore she was sheathed and doubled again in 1791 and this was repeated in 1806, 1815 and 1843. This was the usual method of preparing a vessel for the northern fishery and an extra layer of planks sometimes two layers, fixed to the hull gave protection against the impact of floating ice. Doubling was usually combined with extra beams to fortify the interior of the hull and a massive amount of timber within the bows.

Truelove was of typical eighteenth century design with a pronounced tumble-home to the hull and this together with the extra skin of planks gave her a sturdy well-rounded form, ideal for resisting the pressure of the pack ice. Dimensions prior to lengthening are not known except that her burthen (burden) was 200 tons which rose to 293 tons, and breadth was 27 feet. The quarter galleries and three-quarter length figure of a woman were removed in 1790, while the watercolour by William

Ward executed in 1801 shows a plain stem, all carved decoration having been removed. By 1815 a figure of a man's bust had been installed but this was also removed, sometime before 1844. Capt. Barron tells us that this was done because ice tended to accumulate around it and the overwhelming majority of whale-ships had a plain stem or a simple scroll. The old 'pig-sty' bulwarks with every other plank left out were filled in at the same time because though they allowed water to drain off freely they also made working on deck 'making off' the blubber cold and draughty work.

For eleven years *Truelove* was under the command of Capt. R. Clark until 1795 when George Stephenson sailed her to Oporto before returning under her old master for three more arctic voyages before his retirement at the age of sixty-seven. He only once reached double figures for the whales caught in a season but evidently the return was enough to cover expenses and the vessel would make trading voyages after returning from the fishery. Captain Greenshaw was engaged for the next five seasons and made a series of excellent catches at Greenland, fourteen on his first trip being the highest. After completing the 1803 season on the 22 July *Truelove* sailed for a cargo of wine, armed with the ten carriage guns permitted by the letter of marque she carried. At the beginning of the French wars she had sailed south in the protection of a convoy but for the remainder of the hostilities she was enabled to defend herself. Capt. W. Milner was her next commander and returned from Greenland on 1 August 1804 with the produce of four whales and 1800 seals. The following season was more successful with a catch of nine whales and in 1806 he took *Truelove* on her first voyage to Davis Strait. He caught eight whales and was still able to return before the end of July since in those early days of the straits fishery the main hunting ground was in the neighbourhood of Disco and vessels were not penetrating into Melville Bay and beyond. The next year was disappointing with only two whales and Milner went back to Greenland where although he caught

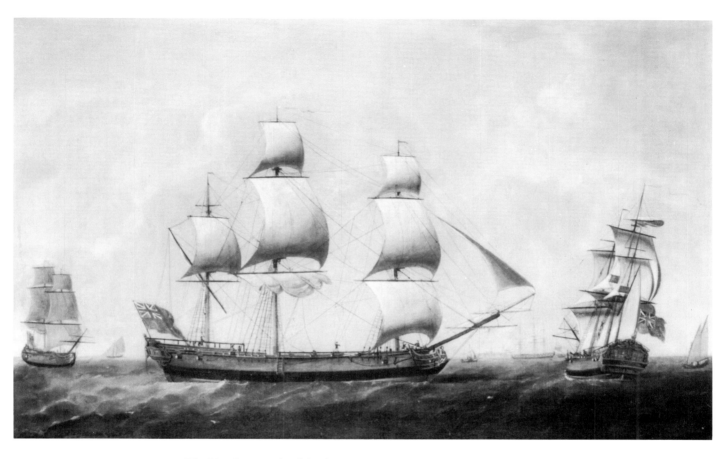

*The **Truelove** a splendid oil-painting by Francis Holman (fl.1760-90)*
made soon after she arrived in England as a prize taken during the American War of Independence.

nineteen 'fish' they must have been small individuals since they only yielded 105 tons of oil. After her season with Milner in 1809 *Truelove* traded to Oporto with Capt. Thomas Foster who then took her on a Davis Strait voyage before handing over to Capt. Henry Watson in 1812.

In 1810 the vessel was in the sole ownership of William Voase, the only son of John Voase, who died aged 70 unmarried and without issue at his seat, Anlaby House, 23 August 1844. Both men served as sheriff of Hull, John in 1784 and William in 1817.

From 1812-20 *Truelove* sailed to Davis Strait with Capt. Henry Watson and then made more Greenland voyages with a Capt. Todd who was lucky enough to avoid one of the worst seasons in the Strait. Fog and strong gales were suffered by both sections of the fleet, but in the confined waters between Greenland and N. America a vessel was more likely to find herself beset and then crushed by a pile-up of ice. Wind and currents drove the floes one against the other so that they rose up in great fractured masses as the pressure increased. Even on the east coast of Greenland the whalers found that the ice extended more than 200 miles further out than usual. Her catch was only three whales and the owners of the *Truelove* evidently decided that the fishery was a bad risk and she went back to trading for the next nine years.

She was bought by Robert King of Sculcoates in 1827 and then by William and Thomas Ward in 1831. William Manger her new captain also took a one eighth share. It was quite usual for the captain to buy into his ship which meant the larger his shareholding the greater his share of the profits of the voyage. Part ownership was both an incentive to a determined application to the whale hunt and a check on recklessness which might put his own considerable investment at risk as well as his future as a ship's master. Other subsidiary shareholders were Henry Preston, a merchant of Sculcoates, and Isaac and John Ward of Bridlington Quay.

Considering the disasters of the previous season it was perhaps a surprising decision to put her back in the fishery and Manger set sail for Davis Strait in the spring of 1831. The vessel was now a bethel ship which meant that there was no fishing on the sabbath and the hoisting of the bethel flag was an open invitation to other whalers in the vicinity to join in Sunday worship. New ownership also brought about a change from ship to bark rig which would enable easier handling with fewer hands.

Manger ended his first season with only three whales but twenty-eight and twenty-two in 1832 and 1833. The yield per whale averaged only seven tons each, indicating that they were considerably undersized. Nine 'fish' were caught in 1834 but his last three voyages yielded only two and a half in total, a whale having been shared with another vessel in the 1835 season. The decline in catches was the result both of a significant reduction of the number of whales and of severe ice conditions during the Arctic summer.

Articles of agreement were signed on 4 April 1831 by the owners of the *Truelove* Thomas Ward (merchant, 12 shares), William Ward (merchant, 16 shares), William Manger (master mariner, 8 shares), Henry Preston (merchant, 16 shares), Isaac Ward of Bridlington Quay (shipowner, 8 shares) and John Ward, also of Bridlington Quay (shipowner, 4 shares). All profits were to be divided amongst them in proportion to their shareholdings and their liability if expenses exceeded income similarly. The whale oil was to be so divided also and each individual to provide the casks to hold this at his own expense "so that the ship's casks may not be removed or interefered with". Whalebone on the other hand was sold by the ship's husband, either altogether or in parcels, at a price agreed by the majority shareholders and profits again divided pro-rata. Thomas Ward was appointed ship's husband and was to have sole direction and management of the vessel. He was paid £42 a year for these services and a commission of £1 per cent on the sale of the whalebone and was to deliver accounts to his co-owners each February.

Captain John Parker took command in 1838 and in

his first season took sixteen whales, but a yield of 100 tons indicates that they were immature, otherwise up to three times the amount of oil could have been expected. Parker did not take a share in the *Truelove* and the portion previously held by Manger was acquired by the principals William and Thomas Ward who were now the only shareholders. In 1839 not a single whaleship was able to penetrate Melville Bay and the next season the Hull fleet consisted of only four vessels the *Truelove, Swan, Comet* and *Abram*. Parker brought two Eskimos to Hull in 1847 under circumstances detailed elsewhere in this volume and two years later he sailed with orders to search for traces of Sir John Franklin. He and Capt. Penny of the *Advice* landed coal and despatches at Cape Hay erecting a pole to act as a marker before sailing south and for home.

In 1850 Parker was delayed by strong winds and owing to the lateness of the season they were unable to get beyond the Frow (Women's) Islands and Upernavik, the northernmost Danish settlement. They crossed over the strait and worked along the west side into the West Water and were temporarily iced in at Cape Hooper with six other vessels. The nearest clear water was some ten miles to the south but eventually the ice broke and the *Truelove* survived unscathed, living up to Barron's approving catch phrase "handy as a cutter, safe as a lifeboat, tight as a bottle, and ready now as of old, to do her duty faithfully".

Returning after the 1853 season the vessel was given a refit during the winter and handed over to William Wells for the next six seasons. Parker returned in 1860 for one more voyage and was succeeded by William Barron for the 1861 season only. Richard Wells took command in 1862 and caught two whales which realised 28 tons of oil and one ton of whalebone. Captain Walker took over in 1863 and a charming reminiscence of George Sorell, an able seaman, tells us that while in Lerwick a salute was fired from their harpoon guns to celebrate the marriage of Edward Prince of Wales, the future Edward VII, to Alexandra daughter of the King of Denmark.

The brief return of Capt. Parker marked the sale of the *Truelove* by Thomas Ward to the Whale and Seal Fishing Co. managed by William Brown and Joseph Atkinson. Throughout 1864-5 the firm was in receivership but in 1866 she was sold to the newly formed Hull Fishing Co. also managed by Brown, Atkinson.

It was probably during this period that *Truelove* was again refitted and nearly came to grief while in Gibsons dry dock. She slipped off the blocks and came to rest on her bilges, but after refloating and replacement on the blocks was found to be quite undamaged. Capt. Wells made two more voyages but she returned in 1867 without a catch. At the start of the season the company had mortgaged the vessel to James Martin, a land agent of Wainfleet, Lincs., for £2000 at 6% interest. Evidently he received the *Truelove* by default after her unsuccessful voyage and Martin sold her to E. P. Maxstead, a Hull merchant and a director of the Hull Dock Co. He was the owner when the *Truelove* made her final voyage to the Arctic fishery, under the command of Capt. Walker who achieved the small return of 9 tons of oil, the produce of 750 seals.

The sturdy old craft was then put into the Norwegian ice and timber trade, Thomas Weatherill being appointed master on 23 March 1869. Maxstead sold her to a Hull corn factor, Castle Kelsey, in 1870 and she continued to sail under the command of Capt. Weatherill. In 1873 *Truelove* sailed for Greenland once more but this time not for the whale and seal fishery but to load a cargo of cryolite, a mineral found only at Ivittuut (Ivigtut) in south-west Greenland, which was a source of sodium and aluminium as well as being used in the glass and ceramics industries. The huge pit which had employed up to three hundred miners was exhausted by 1962, the only significant source of cryolite in the world. The consignment was landed at Philadelphia for the Pennsylvania Salt Manufacturing Co. This was the first time she had been in the place of her 'birth' since being captured by the British. Word

*Ship **Truelove**, a watercolour by William Ward of Hull dated 1801, in the early days of her whaling career. Note the five broadside guns pointing through port holes.*

*Flag presented to Capt. Weatherill of the **Truelove** at Philadelphia in 1873, her first visit since being built there 109 years previously.*

spread through the town concerning the vessel's origins in the port 109 years previously and thousands of visitors came to view her at the Point Breeze moorings. It was even suggested that she be secured for the centennial exhibition, then just three years away, as a relic of the era when the United States of America came into being. This proposal came to nothing but a splendid flag made by Messrs. Hortsmann and Company was presented to Capt. Weatherill on 13 September by Charles Sime on behalf of the Pennsylvania Salt Manufacturing Co. The next day she sailed for England with a return load of petroleum, resin and turpentine.

The flag has survived down to the present and is exhibited in the Town Docks Museum, Hull. Measuring six feet high and fifteen feet long the plain woven wool is decorated with the stars and stripes and in large letters TRUE-LOVE BUILT IN PHILAD^A 1764.

Castle Kelsey defaulted on a mortgage to Edward Smith and John Egginton, bankers, who took possession while *Truelove* was still in America and then sold her to George Dahl and W. J. Sadler, merchants and shipowners of the City of London. She traded between there and Christiania importing ice and timber again. Though she had been regularly refitted and well maintained throughout most of her career the passage of years and the deleterious effects of the repeated changes of ownership since 1860 were evidently making themselves felt. Sailing from South Shields to Tarragona with a cargo of coal she was forced to put into Brixham when several of the crew refused their duties, claiming she was unseaworthy. A Board of Trade inspector insisted that extensive repairs be made before she could be allowed to depart.

Truelove was reported sailing into Liverpool in February 1878 and eastbound past the Lizard the following month. She had been acquired by a certain A. G. Meduru who sold her that year through Mr. F. G. Salmon of Fulham to John Sandilands Ward of London. Lloyds register lists her for the last time in 1889 and in 1897 the great survivor was lying in the Thames being used as a coal hulk. After this date no further record of the vessel can be found and it is surmised that she slowly disintegrated at her moorings and sank into the Thames mud, a sad end to a long and outstanding career, including a record seventy-two seasons in the Arctic fishery. A complete listing of the latter are given in Appendix 8.

Angus Sadler (d.1832)

The outstanding member of a sea-faring family hailing from Cullercoats on the Northumberland coast he was affectionately known as 'But' Sadler from his habit of starting each sentence with this word. Joseph Sadler was a master in the Hull fleet 1802-20 and Angus was mate of the *Manchester* under Peter Sadler. There is some confusion about the relationship of the two men and Peter must have been an elder brother, not his father since he is said to have died at sea in 1794 aged 49. Another Peter Sadler was bosun of HMS *Orion* when Nelson scored his great victory against the French at Aboukir Bay in 1798.

'But' Sadler achieved his first command in 1796 as master of the *Molly* and transferred to the *Aurora* in 1803. The *Molly* was captured and burnt by the French frigate *Syrene* in 1806 but her captain and crew landed safely at Iceland. Aboard the *Aurora* in 1804 Sadler made the all-time record catch of any sailing whaler and brought home the produce of a staggering 44 whales. He was Hull's great rival of William Scoresby Snr. of Whitby and in fifteen voyages from 1796 to 1819 Scoresby obtained 2693 tons of oil and Sadler 2539. Both men fished each year at Greenland and were able through their navigational skill and daring to make good catches despite declining stocks. In 1806 Scoresby penetrated the farthest north in the eastern hemisphere, 86° 30'N which was only exceeded in 1848 by Nils Nordenskiold (1832-1901) the Swedish scientist and explorer.

Sadler also made an outstanding haul of 38 whales in 1808 and 39 in 1811. Master of only two vessels in his entire career he retired at the end of 1817 after twenty voyages without a break, averaging 18 whales a trip. Both vessels belonged to the Eggintons and the *Aurora* was eventually lost at the Davis Strait fishery in 1821 under Captain Thomas.

John Gravill (1802-66)

Born at Gainsborough, Lincs., he was bound apprentice in the whaling trade. This would have been at the age of fourteen or fifteen since the usual period of service was seven years. He was loose harpooner aboard the Gainsborough-owned whaleship *Abram* and then became mate of the *Eagle* in 1833. As mate of the *Harmony* in 1835 he was beset during one of the worst seasons in the Davis Strait fishery. The *Dordon, Isabel, Lee, Mary Frances* and *William Torr* were all lost, nearly a quarter of the Hull fleet, and the remainder managed 32 whales between them.

Gravill's first whaling command was in 1844 as master of the brig *Constantia* of 113 tons employed in the annual harp seal hunt. Owned by Thomas Ostick, a Hull brewer and Edward Chapman, a local druggist, jointly with William Johnson of Gainsborough, she was a small craft and carried only seventeen crew.

After two seasons seal fishing at Greenland, Gravill was appointed master of the *William Ward* a 295 ton vessel fully equipped for whaling. The return for the 1848 season was 225 butts of blubber (70 tons of oil), 10 cwt of baleen, 1 unicorn (ie. narwhal), 1 seahorse (ie. walrus), 8 bear skins and 7510 seal skins. Sadly the following year she was wrecked at Greenland but Capt. Gravill and his crew of 45 were all saved. Caught in a fierce gale on 24 March the starboard side was stove in by floating ice and fatigued and frost-bitten after six days of constant pumping they were taken aboard the *Fairy* of Dundee. The Hull smack *Pledge* of 31 tons, Capt. Joseph Colquhoun, was also lost in the vicinity, near Jan Mayen, on 12 April. The crew of nineteen men, all confirmed tee-totallers, hence the name of their vessel, were rescued by the whaleship *Traveller* and transferred to the *Dublin* of Peterhead for the return trip.

His premature return in the 1849 season led to Gravill being put in command of the *Abram* fitted out with the encouragement and support of Lady Franklin whose husband, the explorer Sir John Franklin, had been missing for some four years. Departing from Hull 12 June it was agreed that while making the search the vessel should engage in whaling and she returned on 21 November with three tons of whalebone and blubber which rendered down into 49 tons of oil. The *Abram* had reached right to the head of Baffin Bay and Gravill became the first European known to have set foot on Ellesmere Island.

Gravill then spent 1850-3 as master of the *Abram* (Mercer and Tidd of Gainsborough) bringing home mixed cargoes of whale and seal blubber and in 1851 some six tons of whalebone. For the next two years (1854-55) he commanded the *Sarah and Elizabeth* an ancient vessel built at Maryland in 1775. She had returned to Hull after whaling out of Australia and had already spent thirty-four years in the Arctic fishery from Hull. Under the ownership of Robert Raikes a baker, and William Brown, the *Sarah and Elizabeth* was lost at Greenland in April 1857 under the command of John Gravill Jnr. who was rescued by his father who had transferred to the *Diana*. After three years in the steam whaler *Chase* and another year in the *Diana* (Whale and Seal Fishing Co.) Gravill spent three seasons, from 1862-4, as master of the *Polynia* of Dundee, one of the fine auxiliary steam whalers built by Alexander Stephens and Co., of that port. He returned to the *Diana* for the 1865 season but sadly was to die in his cabin the next year on Boxing Day 1866, whilst beset in the Arctic. The ship's arrival after fourteen months absence was received by a large crowd who watched in respectful silence whilst the veteran whaling master's coffin was conveyed ashore at the south east corner of the Mytongate lockpit by his faithful harpooners and carried to the waiting hearse.

Gravill had served fifty years in the fishery, every year

Angus 'But' Sadler master of the **Molly** *1796 to 1802 and of the* **Aurora** *1803 to 1817. He died in retirement on 19 July 1832, aged 70. His catch of forty-four whales in 1804 was never surpassed.*

Anonymous portrait of Captain John Gravill Snr. (1802-67). After fifty years in the whaling trade he died in the Arctic at the age of 64.

*Obelisk erected in 1869 by public subscription to the memory of John Gravill master of the **Diana** who died in his cabin 26 December 1866. It was carved in Sicilian marble by the sculptor W. D. Keyworth of Savile Street, Hull.*

from 1844 as master of his own vessel and without a season off. A much respected citizen he was a lay preacher at the Great Thornton Street chapel and a staunch upholder of Methodism. As Gravill's funeral cortège left his house at Mounts Place, Hessle Road, the streets were lined with onlookers all the way to the Hull General cemetery. There his resting place is still marked by a splendid obelisk on which is set a relief plaque of the *Diana* trapped in the ice.

John Gravill Jnr. was master of the *Sarah and Elizabeth* 1856-7 and the *Diana* 1858-60. He afterwards moved to Scotland and sailed in the Dundee whaling fleet.

John Parker Snr. (d.1867)

Parker commenced whaling in 1815 and in 1830 was appointed captain of the *Harmony* owned by Thomas Bell of Sutton. He made an inauspicious start to his career as a whaling master by returning home with a clean ship but this was a bad ice season and out of a fleet of thirty-three Hull vessels six were lost and eight failed to catch a single whale. Parker caught four whales in 1831 and did rather better on his last voyage aboard the *Harmony*, the next season, with eighteen whales. In 1833 he transferred to the *William Lee* a fine ship of 367 tons launched at Hull just two years previously for Lee and Tall, merchants. She was to achieve considerable celebrity in 1839 when she returned from Calcutta after restarting Hull's direct trade with India. Parker made the highest tally of the season with twenty-eight whales and followed it with fifteen in the 1834 season but only three in 1835. He then disappears from the whaling lists until 1838 when he became master of the *Truelove* which by that time was one of only six vessels in the Hull fleet.

During the 1840 season finding the usual route across the North Water blocked by ice Parker followed in the wake of William Penny of the *Bon Accord* (Aberdeen) accompanied by the *Lord Gambier* (Newcastle) and the *Lady Jane* (Newcastle). They found a more southern passage across to the Canadian coast and rediscovered Cumberland Sound, first visited by John Davis in 1585.

In 1842 there were only two Hull whaleships, the *Jane* under Capt. Tather and the *Truelove* with Capt. Parker. Owned by Thomas and William Ward; *Truelove* persevered in the whaling fleet under Parker's command for twenty years. On the 8 July 1852 when the American ship *McLennan* (New London) was crushed in a floe Parker took her captain on board and the crew were split up between the *Orion* and the *Lord Gambier* of Hull and the *Princess Charlotte* of Dundee.

Transferring to the brig *Anne* in 1854 his first year's catch was only 50 butts of blubber and half a ton of whalebone and no details are recorded for the next year. After a year off the *Anne* and Capt. Parker returned to the fishery but again there is no report of the catch and similarly in 1858. After another year off, probably employed in the merchant trade, Parker rejoined the *Truelove* as master in 1860 for his last voyage north. In another poor season she returned with 26 tons of whale oil and 30 cwt of baleen for her owners the Whale and Seal Fishing Co. Only the *Diana* with 30 tons and the *Emma* which had overwintered had better results. The latter brought 60 tons of oil and 70 cwt of baleen, the produce of seven whales.

Parker was a very able navigator and very familiar with the coastline of Frobisher Bay and Cumberland Sound. He showed considerable concern for the local populations of Eskimo whose traditional way of life he had seen eroded by contact with the American and British whalers. Parker never lost a ship and obtained for his owners the best results possible in extremely difficult conditions when whales were scarce and the pack ice troublesome. His son John Parker Jnr. was master of the *Emma* (Thomas Ward) 1855-58 and the steamship *Lady Seale* (Whale and Seal Fishing Co.) 1860-61.

William Barron (1835-1913)

Barron is the only Arctic whaleman to publish a full account of his career and the reader is referred to his *Old*

*John Parker Snr. who had an unsurpassed record of twenty-seven years as a whaling master between 1830 and 1860. He commanded the **Truelove** for seventeen years and it was on board her that the two Eskimos Uckaluk, and Memiaduluk were brought to Hull in 1847.*

Captain William Barron active in the whaling trade 1849 to 1865. Here wearing his uniform as Warden of the Hull Trinity House.

Whaling Days for a whaler's-eye view of the trade from 1849-1865. He was educated at the Trinity House Navigation School and apprenticed to Thomas Ward who placed him in the *Truelove* under the tutelage of Capt. Parker. Barron received £35 for six years' service with an additional 6 shillings as a cabin boy attending to the needs of the captain, mate and surgeon. Arriving at Disco in the Spring of 1849 they went into harbour at Godhavn carrying despatches for the Danish governor and a parcel of luxuries as a gift from the Danish consul in Hull. Here the young man took the opportunity of bartering ('trucking') with the natives and obtained a small model Kayak and a sealskin tobacco pouch. Many such items were obtained by the crew in return for soap and items of clothing.

Promoted to the forecastle for the 1850 season he gives us details of the current rates of pay. A mate received £2.15s. a month, this was the allotment paid to his wife or other dependents at home, supplemented by 7 guineas bounty, 8 shillings per ton of oil, 30s per ton of whalebone and 21 shillings for each 'size' fish, ie. when the largest blade was at least six feet. He also received 10 shillings for planting the first harpoon in the whale. The next in rank, the harpooner, received an allotment of 30 shillings, 7 guineas bounty, 8s per ton of oil, 20s per ton of whalebone and 10s for making the first strike. Boatsteerers were given £2.10s a month, 2s 6d oil money and 5s per ton of whalebone. Much depended on results and if the vessel came home 'clean' the harpooner especially would be short of funds on his arrival home since the allotment would have already been made to his family. The men also had to buy their own supplies of tea, coffee, sugar, tobacco and clothing, some of which could be purchased from the ship's slop chest. In later years the oil money was reduced and a better basic wage was paid.

In his memoirs Barron captures the melancholy of interring a shipmate in the lonely wastes of the Arctic. A harpooner had been killed off Black Hook in 1851 when a whale had capsized one of the boats and they had awaited the first opportunity of burying him on the land.

"All hands were called, and the crews from the other ships invited to be present at the funeral. The scanty soil was only a few inches deep, and his grave was speedily dug with crow bars, for shovels were of no use. The funeral procession was most solemn and impressive. All the ships had their flags at half-mast, and about thirty boats, each containing six men, towed the one in which was the coffin and its occupant slowly towards the land. The doctor read the funeral service, and we covered the wooden shell with large stones, placed in such a position that they did not rest upon it. A wooden headboard with the name, age and birthplace of the deceased, and the ship to which he belonged, marked his burial place. I saw it several years after, and it was in good preservation. I may add that I have seen other headboards, fifty years after their erection, in good condition, although bleached quite white by the weather. Many poor fellows are now resting in this inhospitable and sterile country. No gentle hand is there to place a flower upon their lonely graves".

Barron served in every capacity aboard the *Truelove*, *Anne*, *Emma* and *Diana* from apprentice upwards. He made one voyage only in the whaling trade as master — that was in command of the *Truelove* in 1861. In 1862 and 1863 he was mate of the *Polynia* under John Gravill Snr. sailing out of Dundee. The *Emma* had also been transferred to Dundee from Hull and in 1862 he was mate to Captain Nichol. After retirement from whaling, his last voyage in 1865 was as mate of the *Diana* (John Gravill Snr. master), he joined the fleet of Joseph Gee trading with the continent of Europe. He commanded the ss *Sultan* which was subsequently purchased by Bailey and Leetham, also of Hull.

*Model of **Truelove** by William Barron.*

Barron was her master for eleven years, then was in command of the ss *Empress*, for the same firm, which was disabled by a boiler explosion off Spurn in October 1883. He was later master of the *Kaffraria* which was abandoned in the Elbe after being holed in a collision in 1891. A long and hardworking career was acknowledged by being made an elder brother of the Hull Trinity House of which he was a Warden in 1902 and again in 1908. He died on 28 March 1913 aged 71 and is buried in the Western Cemetery, Spring Bank.

Charles Barron followed him in a maritime career and was an officer of the Wilson Line, a member of the RNVR and like his father was elected an elder brother of Hull Trinity House.

William Wells (1815-80)

Born at Towthorpe, near York, he was apprenticed in 1847 to Captain Jackson of the whaleship *Abram*. He completed his apprenticeship in 1835 and signed as a seaman in the *Harmony*. Wells gained his first command as master of the *Ann* just seven years later trading from Hull to Stettin, Hamburg and Bremen at a time when the whaling trade had slumped and the fleet was greatly reduced. In 1844 the situation had improved and ten vessels departed for Davis Straits with Wells as captain of the *Hebe*, a vessel of 140 tons with a crew of thirty, registered in the name of Robert Bilton, a banker's clerk. No right whales were killed and they returned with only 8 tons of oil the produce of two bottlenose whales and 568 seals. The next season 160 butts of blubber were sent for processing, the produce of 6000 seals, the skins of walrus were also landed. Evidently in both years Wells had concentrated on the harp seal fishery near Jan Mayen and made no attempt to hunt for the Greenland

*Captain William Wells in retirement photographed with his granddaughter. Master of the **Helen** 1844-5, **St. George** 1846-9, **Anne** 1850-3, **Truelove** 1854-0 and 1866-7, **Emma** 1861-2 and **Diana** 1863. After coming ashore he was haven master of Hull and adviser to Benjamin Leigh Smith, Arctic explorer.*

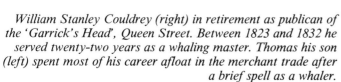

William Stanley Couldrey (right) in retirement as publican of the 'Garrick's Head', Queen Street. Between 1823 and 1832 he served twenty-two years as a whaling master. Thomas his son (left) spent most of his career afloat in the merchant trade after a brief spell as a whaler.

This painting purports to show the fleet of Sir Samuel Standidge in 1769, the **Berry**. **Britannia** and **British Queen** but is derived from a print, published in 1754, after Charles Brooking's picture of the 'Greenland Whale Fishery'. It is therefore an authentic representation of eighteenth century whalers but not of Standidge's own particular vessels.

The **Molly** and **Friends** painted by Thomas Fletcher c.1800. The former is shown in stern and profile view and the latter in the distance. Three whaleboats are linked in line astern towing a dead whale back to the ship. Each boat is inscribed 'Molly Hull' and has a number, alongside the initials 'AS' for Angus Sadler who commissioned the picture. Note the heavy beams over the after part of each vessel which provided a frame for hanging the whaleboats. This clumsy construction was later replaced by davits.

*The fleet of Samuel Cooper, signed and dated R. Willoughby Hull pinx et del. Apr. 1st 1803. From left to right, each shown in two views, **Thomas**, **Brothers**, **Samuels** and **North Briton**.*

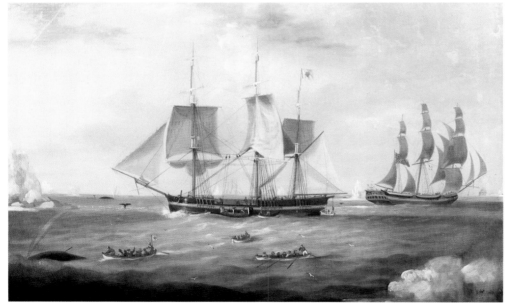

*The ship **Brunswick**, built at Paull (near Hull) in 1814, was in the whale fishery continuously from 1814-34, every year except 1818 commanded by William Blyth. This oil painting, commissioned from John Ward in 1823, celebrates the capture of thirty-six whales, equally the success of William Scoresby Snr. in 1798. Blyth was a devout Christian and the picture originally had a paper label pasted at the top with the words 'Thou God Seest Me'.*

whale. The *Hebe* made a very early return in 1845 arriving in Hull on 12 May. The following year he took command of the *St. George*, a London registered vessel which sailed with the Hull fleet. A small vessel of 158 tons and 34 crew she again seems to have been mainly concerned with the seal fishery though 1½ tons of baleen were recorded in 1848 and ¾ ton in 1849.

Transferring to the *Anne*, a large brig of 256 tons and crew of 42 men, Wells was moderately successful in the four seasons 1850-53 even though his biggest haul yielded only 75 tons of oil and four tons of baleen. From 1854 to 1859 he was master of the *Truelove* and the desperate efforts to try and make a profitable voyage are shown by the inclusion even of polar bear skins in the cargo description. In 1856 Wells brought home two *live* bears which were sold for £35 each to the proprietors of the Hull Zoological Gardens.

Truelove was several times trapped in the ice during the latter season but was released without serious damage; a Dundee whaleship the *Princess Charlotte* was however crushed by the pack. Wells published a lengthy account of the voyage in the *Hull Advertiser* with heavy criticism of Captain Deuchar's crew who had blasted the wreck open and removed a large quantity of spirits. There followed appalling scenes of drunkenness and fighting. One man lay on the ice with his head cut open, another walked on the ice nearly naked and bereft of his senses while another had his eyes nearly gouged out.

After a year in trade Wells sailed north yet again, this time as master of the bark *Emma* owned by Thomas Ward of Hull. 1861 was an extraordinarily good season for this period of the fishery and he captured twenty whales which yielded 166 tons of oil and eight tons of baleen. In contrast she arrived back 'clean' the next season and Wells switched to the *Diana* which was by then in the posession of the Whale and Seal Fishing Co. Three whales yielded 46 tons of oil and 50 cwt of whalebone, the best of the year in a total fleet of four vessels and the *Truelove* returned home 'clean'. He had taken with him his son William Henry Wells then aged

seventeen, who had signed as engineer. A splendid account of this voyage survives in the typescript of a slide lecture which William was to give in after years. There is also a log for the same voyage kept by the surgeon, W. Farr, who included a number of decorative vignettes of the whale hunt, the Eskimo and Arctic scenes. Wells' son had previously sailed with his father in the *Truelove* in 1858 when only a lad of twelve but he was to make his career as a gas engineer and latterly as Chief Inspector of Nuisances (sanitary inspector) in Newcastle where he died in 1908.

In 1864 Capt. Wells commanded the Dundee whaler *Narwhal* and the next year was apparently trading again before returning to the *Truelove*. During the 1866 season only she and the *Diana* sailed for the fishery, the latter being forced to overwinter with such tragic results for her captain and so many of the crew. *Truelove* was the only Hull whaleship for the 1867 season and carried extra provisions on board in the hope of sighting the *Diana*. After returning home 'clean' Wells abandoned the whale fishery and was appointed Hull harbour master. He resigned from his post and retired to the country, dying on 27th April 1880 at Rimswell near Withernsea. A fine headstone in the churchyard there is carved with the scene of a whaler beset in the ice.

William Stanley Couldrey (d.1876)

Couldrey in his first command as captain of the *Duncombe* in 1823 made an excellent catch of twenty-five whales in Davis Strait. He followed this with 10 the following year, a more typical return, and then transferred from the *Duncombe* owned by Samuel Cooper to the *Mercury* of Mercer and Tidd, Gainsborough, but had only modest success and lost his ship at Davis Strait in 1827. Still with Mercer and Tidd he was put in command of the *Mary Frances*, a full rigged ship built at Hull in 1783 and first put in the fishery in 1813. This was the most fruitful period of his career and though returning home 'clean' in the difficult season of 1830 he had caught twenty-seven whales in 1828,

*The ship **Diana**, c.1857, after the installation of her 40 hp auxiliary engine at Earles shipyard. This oil painting by J. Wheldon shows the vessel in three views, bow, stern and port side.*

*The **Diana**, temporarily abandoned by the crew on 2 December 1866, when her destruction seemed certain. In the foreground is the bulky figure of the surgeon, Charles Edward Smith, and his scotch terrier Gyp, who probably provided the sketch on which this oil painting by R. D. Widdas, dated 1867, is based.*

*Loss of the ship **John**, Nathaniel Newham commander 9th July 1821 at Cape York, bearing NE by N. Distance 5 miles, latitude 75°56′N. This watercolour painting, signed William Smith, presumably a crew member, was passed down in the family of Captain Newham.*

Pair of Scrimshaw walrus tusks mainly decorated with characters from the novels of Sir Walter Scott, including Sir Ivanhoe and the fair Rowena.

*The **Mary Frances**, built at Hull in 1753. She first sailed in the fishery in 1813. From 1828 until her loss in 1835 at Davis Strait she was under the command of William S. Couldrey. This painting was commissioned in 1832 after an outstandingly successful season when 29 whales were caught.*

*The **William Lee** in three views by John Ward of Hull. The picture was commissioned from the artist by Capt. Richard Hill (his name is inscribed on the whaleboat) who caught 27 whales in the 1832 season. In the foreground two whaleboats tow a dead whale, while another is being harpooned in the middle distance. Note that the main topsail is backed and the vessel 'hove to' while flensing is in progress. The 'kent purchase' is fastened to a slip of blubber (right) and another slip is being winched up with a 'speck tackle' (left).*

79

twenty-nine in 1832 and thirty-two the following year. To commemorate his bumper catch in 1832 he commissioned from William Griffin a painting of the *Mary Frances* which now hangs in the Town Docks Museum. The vessel was lost in August 1835 in another year of disaster when five of the twenty-three Hull vessels at Davis Strait were wrecked. Couldrey disappears from the whaling lists for several years, perhaps relegated to a subordinate position or transferring to a trader. In 1839 he was appointed master of the *Abram*, another of Mercer and Tidd's vessels, when the Hull fleet was down to only six vessels but he and Capt. Parker of the *Truelove* both returned with the produce of nine whales. The next year the *Abram* arrived 'clean' as did the *Comet* and the entire catch of the Hull fleet of four vessels was only three whales. Couldrey retired from the sea at what was the end of the great period of Hull whaling and became publican of the "Garrick's Head" in Fish Street. He died at the Kingston alms houses, Sculcoates, in 1876.

The Couldreys originated in North Yorkshire and William was born at Thirsk. His own son Thomas was born in Hull and baptised at Holy Trinity Church. After serving in the Baltic trade he became mate of the whaleship *St. George* under Capt. Nicholson in 1853 and himself master of the 190 ton brig *Violet* in 1854 when she was lost at the fishery. The remainder of his career was as captain or mate of various Baltic steamers and in 1874 he was chief officer of the *West Riding* on a voyage to Nagasaki.

The Diana and the Whale and Seal Fishing Company.

The bark *Diana* built at Bremen in 1840, 117ft long and 28ft wide, was purchased from German owners in 1856 and placed under the management of Brown, Atkinson, shipowners and shipping agents. Her owners were a group of thirteen shareholders including both William Brown and Henry John Atkinson as well as her captain, John Gravill Snr. The three major holdings belonged to Thomas Gregson, William Fisher West and Isaac Whitaker.

She sailed to Greenland in February 1856 and returned in May but no details of her cargo are recorded. It was then decided to instal a steam engine, the first major technical innovation in the whaling trade since the introduction of the harpoon gun at the beginning of the century. The engine, installed by Earles of Hull, though only 40 h.p., made her the first ever steam-powered whaleship. Independent of the wind, the *Diana* was able to progress to the whaling grounds and avoid the delays caused by slack or contrary winds. Now converted to ship rig, she arrived at Hull in May 1857 with 140 tons of blubber, 1,300 seal skins and five live seals, the latter no doubt intended for the Hull Zoo. Thanks to the engine which enabled his vessel to maintain position at the ice edge, despite severe weather and a heavy swell, Capt. Gravill was able to stand by the *Sarah and Elizabeth* which foundered in the pack. His son, John Gravill Jnr., and the entire crew were brought safely home.

Evidently the performance of the *Diana* impressed the owners enough to acquire the former cargo-passenger vessel *Sir John Harvey* which entered service in 1858, renamed the *Chase*. Two years later the principals issued a prospectus for the Whale and Seal Fishing Co. and the public was offered £10 shares to raise capital to a total of £7,500, most of which had already been subscribed by the directors, Richard Beckett of Watton Abbey, William Brown, William Fisher Ward, James Daynes, Henry John Atkinson and Thomas Abbey. The company also purchased the steam schooner *Lady Seale* and two sailing vessels, the *Truelove* and *Anne*, all under the management of Brown, Atkinson. The idea was that the steamers as well as working on their own account would assist their companions, by taking them under tow in difficult conditions while the sailing vessels would in turn carry extra coals to ensure that the steamships did not run short of fuel. In the first season the brig *Anne* and *Lady Seale* arrived clean while the *Chase* was lost after being beached for repairs at Button Point. Strong winds drove her bodily onto the rocks but her crew was eventually taken on board the whaler *Narwhal* of Dundee. As her captain John Gravill Snr. ironically observed, the insurance of £16,500 made it the most rewarding voyage made by any vessel of the Whale and Seal Fishing Co. Only the *Diana* and *Truelove* made a catch and returned with 33 cwts of whalebone and blubber which produced 56 tons of oil.

John Gravill Jnr. in command of the *Diana* 1858-60 handed her back to his father for the 1861 season during which he made a quite outstanding trip and arrived home with a "full ship". Twenty-six whales were caught which produced 150 tons of oil and 160 cwt. of bone. Unfortunately the *Anne* was wrecked in Melville Bay, but the *Lady Seale* and *Truelove* between them caught four whales which yielded 173 tons of oil and a quantity of bone.

George Simpson was commander of the *Diana* in 1862 and together with the *Lady Seale* and *Truelove* the produce of twelve whales was brought home. Only four vessels sailed from Hull in 1863, the *Aeolus* and the three remaining vessels of the Whale and Seal Fishing Co. The *Lady Seale* was lost in Melville Bay, the *Truelove* arrived clean and the *Diana* made the modest return of 46 tons of oil and 30 cwts. of bone from three whales.

The *Aeolus* (principal owner Michael Wrangles Clarke) sailed alone from Hull in 1864 and was lost the following season off Iceland. *Diana* was the only other whaler out of Hull in 1865 and returned with the produce of five whales. The Whale and Seal Fishing Co. was reformed in 1866 as the Hull Fishing Co. with most of the same shareholders participating and the *Diana* and *Truelove* were sent north yet again. The latter arrived home on 23rd October having caught two whales, but the ill-starred *Diana* was still in the Arctic, fast in the pack. During July, at what should have been the height of the season, Capt. Gravill was unable to get into Ponds Bay because of heavy ice and so early the next month decided to turn southward heading for home. The *Diana* followed in the wake of the *Intrepid*, commanded by Capt. Deuchars notorious for the *Princess Charlotte* affair in 1856 when his crew went berserk after raiding the spirit casks of the wrecked ship.

Thanks to a superior 60 h.p. engine the *Intrepid* was able to find her way through the loose floes, but the *Diana* was left stranded. Everyone aboard the Hull ship was very bitter at being left behind and complained that Deuchars should have been able to give them a tow or at least spare some coal to supplement her scanty supplies. The epic story of their privations is recorded in *From the Deep of the Sea*, a book based on the journal of the ship's surgeon, Charles Edward Smith, kept during their ordeal in the winter of 1866-67. The captain, John Gravill Snr., died in his cabin on the 26th December and twelve other men were to follow before the *Diana* finally reached safety in the Shetlands.

Most of the crew arrived back in Hull by steamer and Captain Robert Day took over the command for the last leg home to Hull. After bringing ashore Gravill's coffin, the *Diana* was hauled through the Princes Dock into the Queens Dock when at about 12 noon on the 26th April she tied up at her berth oppposite the offices of the Hull Fishing Co. (Brown, Atkinson) in Parliament Street, fourteen months after her departure.

She was subsequently mortgaged to James and Ernest Leetham, shipowners, for £1,500 at 6% and apparently this was defaulted since they were able to sell the *Diana* in December that year to Edward Shepherd Humphrey, H. S. Hodge and Councillor J. T. Robson. After refitting she sailed for Greenland on 10th February 1868 with John Silvey as master and Mr. Hodge on board as an observer.

The Hodge family made a considerable fortune in the oil-seed crushing industry and whale oil was presumably the commodity which was of interest. Staunch supporters of Methodism in 1872 Henry Hodge handed over a £1,000 banknote when he laid the foundation stone of the Primitive Methodist Chapel in Williamson Street.

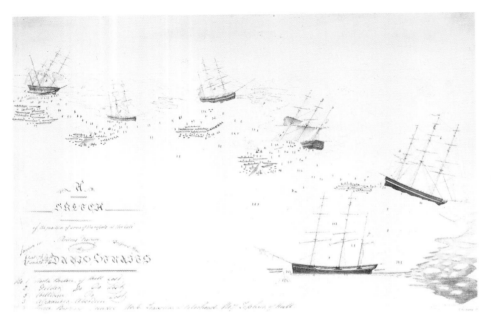

Sketch by Edward Gibson, shipbuilder and amateur artist, of the whaling vessels beset at Baffin Bay, lat. 73° 14' N in the 1830 season. The crews of four vessels have abandoned ship and are camping on the ice. Left to right (a) **Gilder**, *Hull (lost) and the* **North Brit**, *Hull (lost) immediately behind it, (b)* **Alexander**, *Aberdeen (lost), (c)* **Three Brothers**, *Dundee (lost), (d)* **William** *lost, (e)* **Traveller**, *Peterhead, and in the foreground (f)* **Zephyr**, *Hull.*

The **Swan** *and* **Isabella** *by John Ward of Hull c. 1835. Note the distinctive white swan figurehead of the former which she retained from her days as a naval gun brig. A whale is alongside the* **Isabella** *and flensing is in progress.*

The brig **Germanica** built at Gröhn (Hanover) entered the Hull fleet in 1851. After three of his crew died of exposure engaged in the seal hunt in the 1853 season her master, William Birch, was committed to York Assizes accused of manslaughter. He was acquitted and was in command of the **Germanica** when she was lost 19 June 1854. All the crew were rescued and Birch made his last voyage to the fishery in 1855 as master of the **Venerable**.

The **Diana** painted by J. Wheldon c.1857. Two whaleboats move in for the kill while a party of men on the ice are clubbing seals. The last of the Hull whalers, she was lost in 1869.

The *Diana* and the *Truelove* comprised the active Hull fleet this season; the former made a return of 120 seal skins and two tons of seal oil, the latter 750 skins and nine tons of oil. The *Truelove* retired from the fishery and the *Diana* sailed as Hull's sole representative in 1869, this time under the command of Richard Wells. On the homeward journey her engine failed and in difficult weather she was taken under tow off Flamborough Head by the steam tug *Herring Scott* belonging to Whitby. Forced to let go the tow rope off the Bull light, the *Diana* was driven ashore on the Sandhaile flats near Donna Nook. The crew spent several hours clinging to the rigging, the sea washing over them until a lifeboat reached the stricken vessel. All the crew were saved but the *Diana*, the last of the Hull whalers, was a total wreck.

CHAPTER 7
THE ESKIMO AND THE WHALING TRADE

The first Eskimo to be seen in England was brought here in 1576 having been enticed aboard Martin Frobisher's vessel through his fascination with the sound of the ship's bell. He died not long after landing but during the second expedition in 1577 a man, woman and child were brought home and their likenesses were expertly recorded in the drawings of John White who accompanied the expedition.

Still preserved in the Hull Trinity House is an Eskimo kayak complete with a figure dressed in sealskin and furnished with all his hunting equipment. It was given to the house in 1613 by one of the brethren, Andrew Barker, master of the *Heartsease*, a vessel used by Thomas Marmaduke in several of his northern voyages. The kayak, which now hangs from the ceiling in what has become known as the canoe room, is in fact the earliest complete example of such a craft to survive. Every diarist and traveller of note over the last three centuries has given us a description of the 'Greenland man' in his boat which was one of the sights of Hull. John Ray the eminent naturalist described it in 1661 when it was displayed in the Trinity House sail loft and it was recorded by Marmaduke Rawdon, son of a York merchant, in 1666. Celia Fiennes pens us a description in 1697 and another is included in Defoe's *Tour through England and Wales* (first published 1724-6). Thomas Gent, the rather eccentric York printer and antiquary, includes an account in his *History of Hull* (1735) and John Bigland gives us yet another word picture of this curiosity in *The Beauties of England and Wales*, 1812, by which time the canoe had been moved from the sail loft to its present site.

Andrew Barker took command of the *Heartsease* after the leader of the expedition, equipped by a group of Merchant Venturers of London, was killed by an Eskimo spear. Two accounts of the voyage survive one by John Gatonby, also from Hull, and, another by the young William Baffin who was to achieve considerable fame as an Arctic explorer and give his name to the great bay beyond the Davis Strait.

The kayak is not mentioned in either of the contemporary journals but according to tradition it was brought on board with its exhausted occupant who died shortly afterwards. Though brought to Hull in 1613 it seems that it was not until some six years later that steps were taken to display this relic in the house when Edward Fewlis was paid five shillings for carving a head for the figure.

The story of European contact with aboriginal tribes is usually punctuated with reference to economic exploitation, disease, alcoholism and loose morals. On the west coast of Greenland the picture is altogether brighter and the Danes established a series of trading settlements and Lutheran missions which began with the landing of Hans Egede in 1721. The missionary process then lagged somewhat but was given further impetus with the arrival in 1733 of the Moravian brethren, representatives of a protestant sect which had its origins in Bohemia in the fifteenth century. Many natives were converted and attached themselves to the settlements where they were employed in sealing and whaling on behalf of the Royal Greenland Company of Denmark in return for food, clothing and weapons. Their treatment and welfare was strictly controlled by a resident Danish governor and his subordinates who successfully prevented the excesses so often displayed in the contracts between whalers, traders and native peoples in the south sea.

In 1768 Mikak an Eskimo woman and her child were landed in Britain under the care of a naval officer. The mother returned to Labrador but the boy was subsequently installed in the Moravan settlement at Fulneck, near Pudsey, in Yorkshire to train as a

Kayak with figure in the Hull Trinity House brought home in 1613 by Andrew Barker
*master of the **Heartease**. Popularly known as the 'Bonny boatsman'*
a name recorded by Celia Fiennes in 1697.

missionary. Sadly Karpik died, still a young man of fifteen or sixteen years, during an outbreak of smallpox, before he was able to return to his homeland.

In the same year John Grimston Esq. of Kilnwick near Beverley acquired

> "an Esquimaux Indian dress, this ye mans' (ye womans jacket is like this with a tail behind half a yard long and broader then my hand, they have no breeches but boots very wide at ye top come up as high as ye bottom of their jackets, they put their children into ye tops of these when their hands are employ'd) it is quite new but stinks terribly as they have no method of getting ye oyl from it".

This was no doubt added to his cabinet of curiosities and

had been sent up from Portsmouth along with a "sea-cow's" (presumably a walrus is meant) head from the Gulf of St. Lawrence.

The earliest record we have of an Eskimo visiting Hull is from 1815 when Thomas Lund Thompson, a resident of one of the Danish settlements in Davis Straits, was landed at Hull by Captain Watson of the *Truelove*. An announcement was made in the *Hull Advertiser* for 28th September that he would give a demonstration of kayaking in the dock and demonstrate his skill with the bird dart at six live ducks, just as the Eskimo landed at Bristol by Frobisher in 1577 had done.

The natives of Labrador were rather less fortunate than their compatriots across the Davis Straits and in 1847 Capt. John Parker brought an Eskimo couple from Nyatlick (or Niantelike) in Cumberland Sound in an

The 'Bonny Boat' public house Trinity House Lane named after the Eskimo canoe and its figure
which hang in the Trinity House building opposite.
Called the 'Bonny boatsman' in 1810, this drawing by F. S. Smith is dated 1890.

Lecture-Hall, Goodramgate, York.

THE TWO

ESQUIMAUX

OR YACKS,

Male and Female, brought home by Captain Parker, of the Ship *Truelove*, of Hull, from Nyatlick, in Cumberland Straits, on the West side of Davis' Straits,

WILL BE EXHIBITED

On Thursday and Friday, March 9th & 10th,

In the Lecture-Hall, York,

For Two Days only, previous to their return to their Native Country on the 20th Instant.

This interesting married couple, MEMIADIUK and UCKALUK, (whose respective ages are 17 and 15,) are the only inhabitants ever brought to England from the Western Coast. They have been visited by upwards of 12,000 persons in Hull, Manchester, Beverley, Driffield, &c.

THEY WILL APPEAR

IN THEIR NATIVE COSTUME,

With their Canoe, Hut, Bows and Arrows, &c.

From the Manchester Guardian, Jan. 5, 1848.

THE ESQUIMAUX.—Yesterday, we visited in the lecture-theatre of the Mechanic's Institution, one of those outlying varieties of the human family, not often seen in this country,—a young male and female Esquimaux, natives of Cumberland, on the south-west coast of Davis' Straits, in 65° 20 north latitude, and 67° west longitude. They were brought to this country by Captain Parker (of the whaling ship Truelove, of Hull), who, after having made upwards of twenty voyages to that coast, has had his sympathies so much awakened for a people perishing of hunger, that he has brought this couple hither, in order to bring the condition of the tribes throughout the west coast of Davis' Straits (which is British territory) under the notice of our people and government. It seems that while similar tribes of people along the whole of the east coast, or East Greenland, are living in comfort and plenty, under Danish rule, supplied by the Danes with implements of the chase and the fishery, and as happy as external circumstances can make them, the wretched people on the opposite coast of Baffin's Bay—speaking a dialect of the same language, and being to all appearance the same people—are in the most destitute condition; and that chiefly from want of fire-arms and other means of getting food by the chase on sea and land. Thousands of the wretched denizens of British territory on the west side of the bay, are now dependent on the charity of the captains and crews of whaling vessels, for the means of existence; and several of these captains, we learn, distribute amongst these poor polar savages, large quantities of food and clothing every voyage. Captain Penny of Aberdeen, nearly emptied his own clothes'-chest to clothe them; and Captain Parker has expended upwards of £30 in procuring necessaries for them. The history of the two poor young creatures now here, is brief, but striking. Betrothed, as is the custom of the country, when children of four or five years of age, Memiadluk, the husband, is now only 17, and Uckaluk, the wife, only 15 years old. On the Truelove reaching the coast, Uckaluk, having just lost her mother, and being thus left an orphan, and without the means of subsistence (as all the possessions of the deceased are buried in the same grave) had nothing before her but to live as the dogs do, and perhaps to be devoured by them. Won by Captain Parker's long-tried kindness to the natives, she implored him to take her to England. He refused to take her alone, or to take a male and female, unless married. The two betrothed accordingly became man and wife the night before the ship sailed (the male being shorn of his long hair as a part of the ceremony), and were then received, together with Memiadluk's canoe, spear, small tent of ski ns, &c, on board the ship, and brought to this country. They were in the most filthy state, their skin coated with oil or grease, and covered with vermin, and, the girl especially much emaciated by want of food. They were cleansed, and new

sealskin garments given them, and they are now cleanly in habit, washing once or twice every day. They are, even to each other, taciturn; occasionally subject to great depression; but gentle, docile, grateful, and evidently much attached to Captain Parker. Both suffered considerably at first from sea-sickness, and having experienced every attention from Captain Parker, and Mr. Gedney, the ship's surgeon, Uckaluk went to the former with tears in her eyes, and said—"Uckaluk no father, no mother; Captain Parker be her father, doctor be her mother." In their own country these people eat all their food raw, and will devour from 7lb to 8lb or 9lb of flesh daily; and during the voyage they ate quantities of raw leg of beef; but on reaching England they soon learned to eat cooked meat, and though taking 2lb or 3lb at first, their appetites are now not much greater than those of healthy labourers in this country. Being forewarned by Captain Parker, they never touch intoxicating liquors, and their only beverage is cold water. On recovering from sea-sickness, Memiadluk made himself useful on board, helping the sailors in various ways; and on reaching Hull, Uckaluk was taken to Captain Parker's house, and there soon learned to wash clothes, glass and crockery, clean knives and forks, &c. The exhibition is throughout a simple, but interesting one. Both male and female are clothed in a neat dress of sealskin; their stature is low; their colour dark, like that of the quadroon, but with long flowing black hair; their features seem a mixture of the Malay and the African, or in mild, sad expression, resemble the Hottentot. The male gets into his canoe, holds the paddle and poises the spear. A description, from which we have gleaned the above particulars, is given by Mr. Gedney, surgeon of the Truelove; and afterwards Captain Parker explains the condition of the people on both sides of Baffin's Bay, and draws that contrast between the Danish and the British rule, which is so little to the credit of our country. It appears that muskets and ammunition are all that are wanting to place these poor creatures in a condition of comparative comfort; and that the Danes, by doing this, by sending them medical men and missionaries, and building them wooden cabins, have not only increased their comforts, but succeeded in establishing a lucrative trade, taking from them whale and seal oil, and the skins of the seal, the bear, the fox, &c., and sending them guns and ammunition in return. Captain Parker, in seeking by this exhibition to induce the British government to pursue some such kindly policy towards these territorial subjects of Queen Victoria; and as to the two Esquimaux, he is collecting for them with the proceeds of their exhibition, a good stock of these and other necessaries of Esquimaux life, preparatory to their return; and he assures us he shall take them back on his next whaling voyage, leaving Hull about March next.

DAY EXHIBITION, from 2 to 4, ADMISSION, ONE SHILLING. EVENING EXHIBITION at Seven o'Clock, ADMISSION, SIXPENCE. SCHOOLS AND CHILDREN, HALF PRICE.

BROOKS AND LENG, PRINTER, BOWLALLEY-LANE, HULL.

Poster advertising the appearance of Uckaluk and Memiadluk the Eskimo couple brought from Cumberland Sound by Capt. Parker in the Truelove in 1847.

effort to inform the public about their plight. Although Labrador was British territory there was no official presence and the aboriginals were unprotected by any colonial authority.

The result was that the Eskimo tended to suffer many of the disadvantages of association with their European visitors while gaining few of the advantages. An increasing number of whale ships arrived in Cumberland Sound to complete the season's fishing, arriving there either from the North Water and West Water at the head of Baffin Bay or directly across the Strait if Melville Bay was blocked by ice. Parker had himself frequented there for nearly twenty years and he saw that the problems of survival over winter were being aggravated by a growing dependence by the natives on firearms supplied by the whalers. There was a tendency for the traditional skills with the bow to be neglected and without a permanent settlement there was no guarantee of a regular supply of powder, shot and replacement guns.

The Greenland Eskimo in the remoter areas, distant from Danish protection, were not however completely isolated from some of the more unruly elements of the whaling crews. At a meeting of the Hull whaleship owners in 1818 it was reported that men from the *Swan* and the *Eagle* including Captain Brewis had plundered a native dwelling at Four Island Point and then set fire to it. A circular letter was sent to all captains urging them to maintain friendly and considerate treatment of the natives at all times with a recommendation that no boat should go ashore without a responsible officer in charge, no strong liquor should be given and no natives brought back without the consent of the Danish governor.

The two Eskimos from Cumberland Sound,

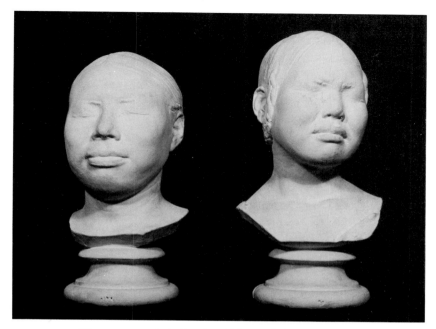

Plaster casts of the heads of Memiadluk and Uckaluk
prepared by W. D. Keyworth, the sculptor.
A head of Capt. Parker was made at the same time.

Memiadluk, and his companion Uckaluk were married, presumably by Parker with his authority as ship's captain, shortly before the *Truelove* began the journey to Hull. They brought with them their kayak and other accoutrements and their welfare was superintended throughout the voyage and their stay in England by William Gedney, the ship's surgeon. As soon as they arrived in port they were vaccinated against smallpox and in order to raise money to help them and their people were exhibited at the Public Rooms, commencing 2nd December. Each was dressed in a new suit of sealskin clothes and Memiadluk busied himself about his boat and hunting equipment.

During their stay they were taken to see a kayak mounted with an effigy of an Eskimo displayed in the museum of the Literary and Philosophical Society and responded with great delight to the wholly unexpected sight. This particular relic had been given to the Society by Sir John Ross and is now to be seen in the Town Docks Museum.

Early the next year they were seen at the Mechanics Institute in Manchester and, shortly before returning home, at the lecture hall in Goodmangate, York. Before taking ship they were invited to meet the wardens and brethren of the Hull Trinity House who presented them with several new guns, ammunition and tools. It is not recorded whether they saw the Andrew Barker canoe and effigy but it seems likely that they did. Captain Parker utilised the money raised from the admission fees paid to view the Eskimos to provide them with yet more firearms and other useful items. Sadly Uckaluk died during an outbreak of measles soon

The three Eskimos,
Tickalicktoo (right), Harbah (left)
and the boy Harkalukjoe,
brought to Hull in 1853 by
Thomas Bowlby and brought
before Queen Victoria at
Windsor Castle.

*Toy Kayak and tobacco pouch of sealskin,
typical of the items which the whalers acquired from the Eskimo
by barter or what they termed 'trucking'.*

after leaving Stromness. The disease had been brought on board by an Orkney man but surgeon Gedney successfully victims back to health including Memiadluk who was landed off Cape Searle with his pile of gifts and found a new wife a few days after his arrival.

Considering the example provided by the long established settlements of the Danes and the commercial success they had achieved in cooperation with the natives it is remarkable how long it took for anyone else to follow suit. The idea of setting up shore bases for whaling and sealing had been mooted by James Clark Ross in 1837, but an American enterprise at Cumberland Sound during 1851-52 was the first attempt. The following year Capt. William Penny, a Scottish whaling master, wintered in Cumberland Sound but stayed aboard his two vessels the *Lady Franklin* and *Sophia* rather than building huts on shore.

John Bowlby, a wine and spirit merchant with the converted revenue cutter *Bee* and schooner *Seaflower*, had made a brave essay in cod-fishing at Davis Strait in 1848. This experience encouraged him to invest in a much more ambitious project in 1853 to establish a trading settlement in Cumberland Sound. Bowlby set sail with the *Bee, Seaflower* and a third vessel the *Wellington* of 25 tons. He succeeded in setting up a house on one of the small offshore islands which he named after himself and a nearby harbour was called Stoneferry. Unfortunately the *Wellington* which was carrying the major part of the timber for construction purposes was lost in Exeter Bay. The crew of five men and a boy never reached the destination but were picked up by a whaler. His enterprise was a failure but Bowlby took on board three Eskimos. Horbah, his wife Tickalicktoo and a child Harkalukjoe. They were looked after by surgeon Gedney who had embarked with the ill-fated expedition and were subsequently brought before Queen Victoria at Windsor Castle as representatives of Her Majesty's most northern territories. They were also exhibited at the Lowther Rooms off the Strand along with their hunting accoutrements amidst a snow scene decorated with a variety of stuffed and mounted Arctic animals. While they were in the capital they were invited to lunch at the deanery in Westminster by Frank Buckland the noted naturalist, who also showed them round the abbey.

> "Among the monuments, that which attracted their attention was the figure of a ship; they also fell greatly in love with a marble anchor. I shall never forget the amazement and excessive delight when they first heard the organ's notes rolling along the aisles."

Back in Hull the native couple and child appeared at the music hall and demonstrated their kayak on the lake in the zoological gardens. They also made an appearance at the De Grey Rooms in York (one shilling admission in the afternoon, sixpence in the evening, scholars and children half price), and at the Mechanics Institute in Pocklington before returning to their home in the distant Arctic. They were apparently the last of their race to visit Hull on board a vessel of the local whaling fleet.

The close attention throughout their stay of Mr. Gedney who acted as their chaperone and interpreter suggests that this was another attempt to raise funds to provide help for the Eskimos of Cumberland Sound as Capt. Parker had done five years previously. Bowlby had evidently taken Parker's strictures to heart and had planned setting up his trading station on the lines of the Danish settlements. A number of English and Scottish whalers were to overwinter there in subsequent seasons but none of them established a permanent site and merely anchored their vessels adjacent to the Eskimo villages and lived on board ship.

CHAPTER 8
HULL WHALING: THE FINAL PHASE.

From 1843 to the final year of 1869 thirty-eight vessels left the city and fourteen were lost or over a third of the total. These were a motley array of craft ranging from ships and barks to brigs, schooners and even a sloop, a ketch and a smack. Numbers reached another peak in 1846 with a fleet of fifteen and there was a sustained level of activity for the next seven years, when the entry dropped from thirteen in 1853 to eight the following year. Then in 1856 there began a new and concerted effort to breathe life into the trade with the purchase (from Germany) of the *Diana* which before the start of her second season in 1857 was fitted with a 40 hp steam engine at Earles shipyard on the Humber to make her the world's first steam-powered whaler.

Several iron-hulled steamers were tried in the fishery in 1859 namely the *Corkscrew, Gertrude* and *Emmeline*, the last belongng to Zachariah Pearson and John Coleman. In the freezing conditions of the arctic the iron plates lacked the resilience of a wooden hull in encounters with the pack ice and all of them suffered considerable damage and were not sent north again. The *Labuan*, belonging to Bailey and Leetham, the great rivals of Thomas Wilson's steamship company and commanded by John Wilson, was slightly more successful with a yield of 125 tons of oil, but this was her only trip to the fishery and she was put back into normal trade. William Leetham, principal in the firm, had commanded the *Corkscrew*, which 'brought five seals and lost her screw' while the *Emmeline*, Capt. Matthew Brown, returned home clean.

The value of the seal catch increased as a proportion of the return on the voyage as the Greenland whales became even scarcer. To increase productivity and extract the most profit from the capital invested in ships and equipment the idea developed of setting up permanent stations in the Arctic. The seal and whaling hunting continued until the onset of winter made further efforts impossible and could resume immediately after the Spring thaw. In addition the catch was boosted by employing in the hunt the local population of Eskimo who received clothes, tools and various store goods as payment. They were also employed in salting down the seal skins and 'making off' the blubber which was by this time collected in iron tanks fitted below decks instead of in barrels. A journal written in 1859-60 aboard the *Emma* by one of the boatsteerers Albert Johnson Whitehouse, preserved in the Town Docks Museum, is a unique record of a Hull whaler (deliberately!) overwintering in the Davis Strait. The *Emma* was accompanied by a small steam tender the *Isabel* which carried extra crew and provisions and was available to tow the parent ship (not provided with an engine) when the wind failed; without such help the task was a back-breaking one of towing her with a line from the capstan to an anchor buried in the ice pack ahead, a process known as 'warping'.

The *Isabel* it seems returned to Hull in June of 1859 with at least some of the produce for that season before going back to accompany the *Emma* home the following year.

Out of the thirty-eight vessels in the post-1842 fleet only a handful had been active before the near extinction of the Hull fishery. The *Abram* resumed her whaling career in 1844-53 before transferring to the Kirkcaldy fleet in 1855 and the *Jane* sailed from 1843-46 when she also went to Scotland to be based at Bo'ness. The *Venerable*, built at Scarborough in 1798, sailed in the fishery from 1809-37 returning to Greenland in 1852. The *Sarah and Elizabeth* another ancient craft, built in 1775, returned to Hull for entry in the fishery in 1844 before finally being lost in 1857 under the command of Capt. Gravill Jnr. Of all these remarkable old craft the *Truelove* was outstanding and retired from

ARRIVAL OF

The Swan

From Davis' Straits. 25 Lives Lost.

Yesterday, Monday July, 3rd, in consequence of intelligence of the Swan having made the Humber, many thousands assembled at Southend, and were gratified with the sight of the long-lost vessel, whose reappearance was regarded as a sort of resurrection. On nearing the Humber Dock Basin, three loud and hearty cheers were given by the assembled multitude on shore, and answered from the Swan; this was at five o'clock, and during the two succeeding hours which elapsed whilst passing through the New and Junction Docks, until she was safely moored on the north side of the Old Dock, the thousands of spectators who thronged all the shipping and both sides of the docks, saluted her with many a cheer, appeared to suffer no abatement.

The survivors of her crew, including Captain Dring and his two sons are all in tolerable health; the mate and one or two others look remarkably well but the majority are still rather thin. No words can well describe the privations and sufferings to which the men have been exposed. The crew of the swan originally consisted of 48 men, 24 of whom, including the captain and officers, sailed from Hull, and 24 were obtained at Shetland; of the Shetlandmen 11 have died, of our townsmen 7, and two others from Grimsby, while of the six who were received from the wreck of the Margaret, of London, but one survives. But for an unfortunate expedition, in which a

party of men endeavoured unsuccessfully to reach a Danish settlement, the surgeon is of opinion that no more than 12 persons would have died, and of those who died of scurvy it is proper to observe that their end approached very fast, when their spirits began to fail them after the melancholy affair.

During their confinement in the ice, divine worship was conducted every Sabbath, in a most orderly and impressive manner, by a pious Shetlander, the whole ship's company engaging heartily in the service The Swan has three fish, about 30 tuns ; twenty of the Duncombe's men have arrived with her ; the Duncombe has four fish, 60 tuns. The ships were parted in the Western ocean, about a fortnight ago, in lat. 53 N , and long. 40 W., since which they have not seen each other, but the arrival of the Duncombe is daily expected. We intend to recur to this subject next week, by which time we shall be able to give further and deeply-interesting details of this most hazardous voyage.

The following are the names of the men lost—Thomas Haller, Henry Judge, Robert Derby, Robert Collier, Daniel Knight, W. Walker, John Nuttal, John Stocks, R. Brady, (Englishmen), Gifford Wenwick, John Morra, Laurence Duncan, James Jameson, John Johnson, Magnus Harrison, James Moore, Peter Hunter, Thomas Hewson, William Harper, W. Bainton, James Jameson, Alex. Anderson, (Shetlandmen). The last five men belonged to the Margaret of London ; Mr. Stoddard, the mate, being the only surviving one out of the boat's crew. There is very little hope of a north passage this year.

The wife of one of the men belonging the Swan, who anticipated that her beloved husband would not again present himself before her, was on the Sunday last united in the bonds of holy matrimony to her love-stricken swain. On Monday, on hearing of the arrival of the vessel, and the safety of her first husband, she made a precipitate retreat into the country, where for aught we know, she yet remains.

WESTON HOWE, PRINTER and BOOKBINDER, 33, LOWGATE, HULL.

TO BE

SOLD by AUCTION,

BY MR. T. B. MORLEY,

AT THE EXCHANGE, HULL,

On Tuesday, Feb. 17, 1835,

AT TWO O'CLOCK IN THE AFTERNOON,

ALL THOSE

$\frac{56}{64}$th SHARES

OF THE

GOOD FISHING SHIP

EAGLE,

OF HULL,

Register 290$\frac{80}{94}$ Tons,

With the like Shares of all her Casks. Boats, Lines, and other Fishing Stores, in good Condition.

INVENTORY.

Standing and Running Rigging Complete, one Spare Top Mast, one Spare Jib Boom.

Two Bower Anchors	Seven Gun Ditto
Two Kedges	Three Beard Ditto
Six large Ice Anchors	Two Sea Horse Ditto
Two small Ditto	Twenty-four Lances
One Chain Cable	One Gun Ditto
	Nine Blubber Knives
	Six Tail Knives
One Seven-inch Warp	Eight Chopping do.
One Six-inch Ditto	Eight Strand do.
One Five and half inch Ditto	One Nose Knife
Two pairs Chain Topsail Sheets	Nine Spades—Four Spike Hooks
	Nine Pairs Closh Hooks—Four Closhes
	Six Pairs Closh Pins—Ten Pairs Spurs
Three Jibs	Three Ice Saws—Seven Boat Axes
One Flying Ditto	One Ice Axe
Three Foresails	One Drill
Five Fore and Maintopmast Sails—one new	Ten Prickers—Twenty-four Pick-Hooks
Five Fore and Maintopgallant Sails	Eighteen Seal Clubs
Two Mainsails	One pair each Chain, Nipping, and Shake Hooks
One Mainstay Sail	One Toggle
One Middle Staysail	Two and half sets Bone Gear
Topgallant Ditto	Three Bone Handspikes
Two Foretopmast Stay Sails—one new	Two Boat's Davits and Chocks
Two Mizens	Two Dozens Boat's Blocks
One Mizen Stay Sail	Three Boat's Winches and Standards
One Mizen Top Sail	Three Dozens Boat's Oars
One Maintop Gallant Sail	Eight Skeeds
Twelve Steering Sails	One Cant Fall
Three Royals	Two Spike Falls
	One Spike Trough
	Two Spike Blocks
About 105 Tuns Casks	One Guy
	Seven Natch Blocks
	Sundry Truss Hoops
Seven Whale Boats	Five Steering and one Hanging Compass
Fifty-two Whale Lines	Three Telescopes
Sixty-three Hand Harpoons	Seven Time Glasses
	Medicine Chest
	One Gun

☞ *For further particulars and Inventories, apply to Messrs. HOLDEN and GALLOWAY; Solicitors, Hull ; or to the Auctioneer.*

GODDARD AND BROWN, PRINTERS, PACKET-OFFICE, LOWGATE, HULL.

the fleet in 1868 after serving no less than seventy-two seasons in the fishery.

The structure of the Hull whale fishery was substantially different in the second phase. Instead of being dominated by the great merchant families such as the Eggintons, Coopers and Boltons the enterprise was on a greatly reduced scale and in the hands of a lower echelon of merchant traders, shop-keepers and artisans. The one major enterprise which stands out is the Whale and Seal Fishing Company active from 1860-66 and though not a signal success the managers Brown, Atkinson still continued in charge of the Hull Fishing Company its successor, operating only two vessels, the *Diana* and the *Truelove*.

Amongst a number of small craft the Hull fleet briefly included the *Friends*, a schooner of 41 tons which returned with the produce of 400 seals in June 1848. A press announcement stated that she was especially built for the sealing trade but she had been launched from a Hull yard in 1808 and only sailed to Greenland the one season. The *Friends* was owned by John Carter of Thorne, a master mariner who sold her in August 1848 to Robert Gardam, described in the custom register as a joiner and builder, who presumably used her in the coasting trade. The Ketch-rigged *Swallow* of 158 tons (owned by Benjamin Pickering, draper; James Simpson, colour manufacturer; Samuel Lowden, grocer; Robert Martin, gentleman;

and Thomas Lee Jnr, her captain) made five voyages to Greenland but was wrecked in 1849. In the same year the smack *Pledge*, the tiniest craft to sail in the Greenland fleet, was also wrecked. She was a mere thirty tons and unique in being manned solely by teetotallers! Owned by Richard Vivian, sailmaker and smackowner, it seems that seals and perhaps cod fish rather than whales were the intended quarry. In 1848, the previous year, Richard Bowlby, victualler and brewer, had sent the cutter *Bee*, and the schooner *Seaflower*, to Davis Strait, which had returned with 1200 cod, three tons of halibut and four tons of cod liver oil.

A number of the vessels sailing out of Hull were in fact registered elsewhere. The *St. George*, Captain William Wells, in London and the *Rose* and *Gertrude* in Grimsby. The *Lady Seale* though on the Hull register as a trading vessel from 1843 was transferred to London in 1857 and her whaling career which began in 1860 ended with her loss in 1863.

We have already referred to the increasing importance of the seal catch and on a number of occasions whalers made a double voyage, first embarking in pursuit of the harp seal and then on to the Davis Strait fishery. There were a number of variations, the ship might carry straight on to Davis Strait after the Greenland sealing season was over, in which case she would have had to be well provisioned and fully equipped for both endeavours at the time of her departure from Hull. Alternatively she would return to Shetland or Orkney after the Spring sealing to reprovision for the whale fishery or again the vessel might return to Hull before setting out on the long outward voyage, the captain and perhaps most of the crew being changed.

The most comprehensive account of life aboard a Hull whaling vessel at this period comes from the pen of Charles Edward Smith, surgeon aboard the *Diana* in 1866, and published in 1922 as *From the Deep of the Sea*. It records the appalling hardships suffered by all on

*Anonymous watercolour of the whaleship **Fame** owned by William Scoresby Snr. of Whitby;*
she sailed with the Hull fleet under his command from 1820 to 1823
but only in the latter year was she actually registered in Hull.
*The **Fame** was destroyed by fire at Orkney during this same season.*

board when the *Diana* was beset and forced to overwinter. She had almost been lost off Jan Mayen Island seeking harp seals on the pack ice, but eventually returned safely to Lerwick to take on water and provisions before proceeding to Davis Strait. Although Right whales by then were very scarce even a small catch of a handful of animals could be profitable. The demands of the fashion trade for whalebone (baleen) which was turned into corset stays, supports for crinolines and used to make artificial ostrich feathers pushed its price to some £700 per ton. Attempting to make the return voyage, the *Diana*, with the blubber of two whales and half a ton of whalebone, was unable, even with the aid of her auxiliary engine, to force a way through the pack which had begun to pile up early in the season. The Captain, John Gravill Snr. a veteran of sixty-four who had been in the trade for fifty years since he joined as an apprentice, decided to drive her into the pack with the hope that she would eventually be released in the Spring thaw. This is what in fact happened. She drifted slowly southwards during the winter and was ultimately released on the 17th March 1867 to make a very rapid passage across the Atlantic and make a landfall at Ronas Voe in Shetland, despite most of her crew being disabled through scurvy and frostbite. The captain and twelve men, a quarter of the total complement, died on this voyage which finally demonstrated to the shipowners of Hull that there was no real future for the traditional whale fishery and this local industry which had begun in earnest more than a hundred years before was all but dead. Only one vessel sailed from Hull in 1867, everyone apparently awaiting news of the *Diana* before making decisions for the future. In the following year only the *Diana* and the *Truelove* set sail.

The total return of the 1868 season was eleven tons of seal oil and 870 seal skins with the result that the *Truelove* was withdrawn and the *Diana* departed by herself in the 1869 season as the only Hull entrant to the fishery. On the 19th October homeward bound she was

*Joseph Dean was a Hull whaling master for ten seasons between 1835 and 1847, commanding the **Sisters, Duncombe** and **Riby Grove**, all belonging to different owners.*

driven ashore near Donna Nook on the Lincolnshire coast in a storm and was a total wreck, the final curtain for Hull's once great whale fishery. The first warning signs had come as early as 1821 but the sequence of disasters in the 1830s really set the trade on its downward spiral. Briefly the introduction of steam had injected a new impetus but this should have been followed

Scrimshaw plaque in lid of sailor's ditty box.
*The position 71° 26°N probably indicates where the **Riby Grove** was lost in 1838.*

up by investment in new and more powerful steamers specially built for the fishery. Instead a ragbag collection of steamers converted from the mercantile service and numbers of small and totally inadequate brigs and schooners made up the bulk of the fleet.

In contrast the Scottish ports, in particular Peterhead and Dundee, invested heavily in a new breed of purpose-built steam vessels and continued to send large fleets to the arctic for many more years. The emphasis was increasingly on sealing and a mixture of the smaller whale species. 1908 saw five vessels venturing to Davis Strait, two to Greenland, one to Hudson Bay, all from Dundee. The outbreak of the Great War brought the northern fishery to an end. It was now the age of factory whaling in the southern oceans an industry which has brought the threat of extinction to the Blue whale and ravaged the populations of all the great whales.

The 'Full Ship' public house at 10 North Walls, it was renamed the 'Royal Sovereign' in 1851.
A 'full ship' was one with its hold well filled with blubber and bone and confident of a profitable voyage.
*Other licensed premises named in connection with the whaling trade were the 'Ship **Molly**', Dock Street, the 'Whale Tavern',*
High Street and the 'Splaw bone', sometimes called the 'Blade bone' in Wincolmlee.

*Christopher Tait an apprentice aboard the **Diana** when beset in 1866-67.*
*He subsequently made fourteen more Arctic voyages and was the last survivor of the **Diana** crew.*
He died at Aith in Shetland aged ninety-four on 29th February 1940.

CHAPTER 9
SPERM WHALES, MELVILLE AND MOBY DICK

The extent of Hull's contribution to the whale fishery in the South Atlantic and Pacific was insignificant when compared to the effort in the northern seas. A handful of vessels the *Albion, Phoenix, Edward* and *Minerva* are known to have sailed to the south before 1800, but the major investment was based in London. The frantic speculation which led to the financial crisis known as the South Sea Bubble had much to do with the promise of rich returns from the whalers in the southern oceans.

Only one logbook is known to survive of a Hull South Sea vessel, the *Comet* which departed in 1812 and after rounding the Horn put into the port of Telquana on the Peruvian coast. There she became involved in a revolution and was detained for over a year. The considerable store of muskets, powder shot and artillery carried for defence on the high seas during these last years of the Napoleonic wars proved irresistible to the local rebels. After her eventual release whaling continued off the Peruvian coast and the Galapagos islands while the captain, Abel Scurr, who had been sick for some time took to his cabin and finally died. The ship put into Callao where he was duly buried in the churchyard of St. Domingo, Bonavista. In the mean time back in Europe Waterloo had been fought and won by the allies ending the interminable French wars and the *Comet*, homeward bound, gained the first sight of home when the Lizard point came into view on 3 December 1815. They arrived back in England with the produce of 38 whales, sperm whales and others, making 1115 barrels of oil. Apart from the captain there had been three deaths including one man who had fallen off the fore-topmast.

The *Comet* originally built at Rotherhithe in 1781

returned to general trade and was then active in the northern fishery from 1823 to 1840 without interruption. She survived the disastrous seasons of 1830, 1831, 1835 and 1836 when so many vessels were lost or severely damaged owing to the ice conditions.

The *Sarah and Elizabeth*, a veteran of the Arctic from 1784 to 1813, was later sold to London owners and in 1823 made her first voyage to the South Sea fishery. Sailing directly from Hull in 1836, though registered in London, she spent the next six years based in Australia principally involved in whaling. Arriving back in Hull in 1844 this game old ship, built in North America in 1775, returned to the Arctic fishery and was eventually lost at Greenland in 1857 under the command of Captain John Gravill Jnr. after a career afloat of 82 years!

The Sperm whale which was the most keenly sought of the great whales in the southern oceans is occasionally seen in the north. Lone bull sperm whales, generally thought to be old animals which have separated from the groups or schools in which they usually travel, periodically appear in the North Sea and strandings on the English and European coastlines have been reported over several centuries. An example which washed ashore at Tunstall on the Holderness coast in 1825 was set up in the grounds of Burton Constable Hall near Sproatley. Though now only a scatter of bones obscured by grass and weeds it has been immortalised by Herman Melville in that epic novel of the great white whale *Moby Dick*, first published in 1851:-

"Moreover at a place in Yorkshire, England, Burton Constable by name, a certain Sir Clifford Constable has in his possession the skeleton of a Sperm Whale but of moderate size, by no means of the full-grown magnitude of my friend King Tranquo's. In both cases, the stranded whales were originally claimed by their proprietors on similar grounds. King Tranquo seizing his because he wanted it; and

Sperm whale which washed ashore on the Dutch coast at Beuer, 13 January 1610.
An engraving after a drawing by Jan Sanreadam; the artist in a cloak
is seen with his back to the viewer in the left foreground.

Sperm whale washed ashore at Tunstall in April 1825.
Claimed by Sir Thomas Clifford Constable, Lord Paramount of the Seigniory of Holderness,
the skeleton was mounted in the grounds of Burton Constable Hall by Edward Wallis, a Hull surgeon.

Sir Clifford, because he was lord of the seigniories of those parts. Sir Clifford's whale has been articulated throughout; so that like a great chest of drawers, you can open and shut him, in all his boney cavities —spread out his ribs like a gigantic fan — and swing all day up on his lower jaw. Locks are to be put upon some of his trap-doors and shutters; and a footman will show round future visitors with a bunch of keys at his side. Sir Clifford thinks of charging twopence a peep at the whispering gallery in the spinal column; threepence to hear the echo at the hollow of his cerebellum; and sixpence for the unrivalled view from his forehead."

The skelton was articulated and mounted on a metal armature by Edward Wallis, surgeon and lecturer in anatomy and pathology of the Hull and East Riding School of Anatomy and Medicine, established 1831. He was the son of Edward Wallis Snr. commercial traveller and later partner of Crackles and Horncastle, whalebone manufacturers. Melville's fantastical description is typical of the way he teases and pokes fun at the learned authors of his sources, in this case Thomas Beale author of *The Natual History of the Sperm Whale* (1839), and elaborates his raw material into something satirical and strange.

Generally whales and sturgeons were declared royal fish and became the prerogative of the crown, but in several localities the local potentates traditionally had the right to take such animals. This was the case in the palatinate of Durham, where the prince bishop laid his claim, and also applied to the Lords of Holderness. Sir Thomas Constable as Lord Paramount of the Seignory of Holderness accordingly took his due and ordered the

*The whaleship **Pequod** after fitting out in St. Andrew's Dock in 1954
for the film of Moby Dick starring Gregory Peck. Built as a topsail schooner in 1870
it was converted to represent the **Hispaniola** in the film of Treasure Island before being converted
into Capt. Ahab's South Sea whaler.*

MERMAID.

By Permission of the Worshipful the Mayor.

MR. WHATEMAN

Respectfully informs the Inhabitants of Beverley & its Vicinity,

THAT THE WONDERFUL

FISH,

Supposed to be of the Species of the

MERMAID,

From its perfect resemblance to the

Human Figure,

Which was Caught a few Weeks since by the Crew of the Davis' Straits Ship, Mary Frances,

WILL BE EXHIBITED

FOR FOUR DAYS ONLY,

At a House adjoining the WHITE SWAN, in the

MARKET-PLACE, BEVERLEY.

——*oooooooo*——

ADMITTANCE. TWOPENCE.

——*oooooooo*——

This very extraordinary FISH has given rise to much speculation as to the real species to which it belongs, as from its singular appearance, and strong resemblance to the features of the Human Figure, many venture to assert it has some affinity to the MERMAID, while others think it a species of the SUN FISH: at all event it will be gratifying to the Public and to the Naturalist, to have an opportunity of beholding another of the Wonderful Works of the Creation, with which the fathomless deep abounds, at a very trifling expense, previous to its being sent to the British Museum.

T. PROCTER, Printer, North-Bar-Street, Beverley.

*This 'mermaid' was either a seal or a walrus which the crew of the **Mary Frances** would know full well. Polar animals became more familiar to the local citizens after the opening of the Zoological Gardens on Spring Bank in 1840.*

Whalebone arch formerly on the Burton Constable estate.
Note that the hinge portions of this pair of jawbones
(or of another set) have been cut off and used as supports.

the Eskimo kayak given by Capt. Ross referred to above. At the time Melville was writing his most famous novel the material was housed in the old Assembly Rooms, Kingston Square, but soon to be moved to the Royal Institute, built jointly by the Literary and Philosophical Society and the Subscription Library and opened by Prince Albert in 1854.

The most important of the whale skeletons was that of a Blue whale washed up at the mouth of the Humber in 1835. Published in 1847 it was the first of the species to be scientifically described and therefore became the type specimen of all Blue whales. Like the Burton Constable whale it was also assembled and articulated by surgeon Wallis. It remained in the Royal Institute until 1935 when Thomas Sheppard and Dr. A. C. Hardy, then professor of Zoology and Oceanography at University College, Hull, arranged for it to be placed in the national collections at the Natural History Museum, South Kensington. In return a complete skeleton of a female North Atlantic Right whale was placed in Hull's Fisheries Museum at Pickering Park and following its closure in 1974 it was transferred to the Town Docks Museum where it is the centre piece of the whaling gallery. Another large whale, 101ft long, and most certainly a Blue whale was reported in the Humber in the *Gentleman's Magazine* for September 1750 (p.426).

Given the literary reference to Hull in *Moby Dick* it is particularly appropriate that when the film was made starring Gregory Peck, as Captain Ahab, the vessel used to represent the *Pequod* was actually fitted out in the city's fish dock. It arrived in the guise of the *Hispaniola* having previously been used in the film of Treasure Island and was duly transformed into a whaleship by craftsmen in the firm of Industrial and Maritime Riggers. The action sequences with the quite remarkable radio-controlled whale were subsequently filmed in the Irish Sea, a long way from the balmy southern climes which were the natural home of the memorable tattooed figure of Queequeg the native harpooner.

skeleton to be prepared for display on his estate.

It is also of special local interest that Melville's passage on the Burton Constable whale is preceded by a reference to the museum of the Hull Literary and Philosophical Society. "There is a Leviathanic Museum, they tell me, in Hull, England, one of the whaling ports of that country". The collections were by no means solely made up of whale skeltons but these were amongst the largest and most striking objects on display alongside a multifarious assemblage of natural history material and items of local interest, including

CHAPTER 10
THE POLAR TRADITION

The early exploration of the northern seas and the part played by Hull seamen such as Thomas Marmaduke, Andrew Barker and Luke Fox are described in the earlier pages of this book. Many unknown whaling masters, especially Dutch and English, as well as the Danes establishing their outposts in Greenland, played a vital part in increasing our detailed knowledge of the northern regions. The Scoresby's of Whitby did much to map the east side of Greenland and Scoresby Sound is an indication of their contribution. In 1806 the intrepid William Scoresby Snr., master of the *Resolution*, with his son William Scoresby Jnr. as master, reached the latitude 81° 30' North, within 510 miles of the pole. He returned home with a cargo which produced 216 tons of oil making the voyage a considerable commercial success as well as a fine feat of seamanship. It was Scoresby Snr. too who is credited with the introduction of the barrel crowsnest, which for the first time gave protection to the whalers lookout. The research vessel *William Scoresby* was named after the younger Scoresby, who laid the foundations of Arctic science. Built in 1926 at Beverley shipyard it was used for survey work in Antarctica and attempts to plot whale movements by implanting markers.

Capt. Ross chose a Hull-built vessel, the newly launched *Isabella*, for his first attempt to discover the North West passage and was with great fortune rescued in the self-same craft in 1833 after the loss of the *Victoria*. The expedition party survived mainly thanks to the provisions in the form of large tins of meat and vegetables which had been left at Fury beach, Prince Regent inlet, where Parry had abandoned the *Fury* in 1825.

The cache of tins was found intact with no trace of corrosion and examples of two of these are in the Town Docks Museum. Even in 1911 eighty-seven years after they were delivered from Mr. Donkin's factory at Bermondsey the contents were found to be in edible condition.

Humphreys continued fishing for another month and Ross and his companions arrived in Hull on 15 October when he was greeted by the Mayor and representatives of the Corporation, Hull Trinity House and the Philosophical Society and many more town worthies before embarking for London in a coasting steamer.

Ross was elected as honorary brother of the Hull Trinity House on 2 November 1833 and in the same month accepted membership of the Hull Literary and Philosophical Society.

Thomas Wilkinson Wallis (b.1821) the celebrated wood-carver remembered as a boy seeing the polar explorer walking down Charlotte Street dressed in the bear's skins he and his men had made into clothes during their long imprisonment in the far north.

Captain Humphreys at a dinner given in the Vittoria Hotel on 23 July 1834 was presented with a silver cup engraved with a representation of the boats of the *Isabella rescuing the crew of the Victory*. It was inscribed

> "Presented by the subscription of upwards of one hundred of his fellow townsmen, to Capt. Richard Wallis Humphreys, of the *Isabella*, Hull whaler, in testimony of his having rescued Captain Ross R.N. and his enterprising companions, from their perilous situation in the Arctic regions, on the 26 August 1833."

Humphreys was the nephew of the gunsmith George Wallis Jnr. and with the money inherited from his uncle's estate he purchased his own ship which he named *George Wallis*. In 1842 she was wrecked off Sumatra bound from China to Peru, though Captain Humphreys, his son Robert and all the crew were saved.

Captain John Ross and his exploration party discovered by
*Capt. Humphreys of the **Isbella**, 26 August 1833.*

He was appointed sailing master of HMS *Crocodile* in 1847 for her voyage to the Hudson Bay settlements with a detachment of troops. Retirement must have followed soon after and he died at sea as a passenger homeward bound from South Africa on 2 June 1853.

The *Hecla* (375) used by William Edward Parry in his expeditions of 1819, 1821-23, 1823-25 and 1827 was launched at Hessle Cliffs, sometimes known as North Barton, by Hawkes and Co. Built in 1815 as a bomb vessel it had very strong timbering to withstand the stresses of shooting a large mortar from within its hull. She survived the rigours of four excursions into the Arctic and was sold out of the service in 1831.

In May 1845 Sir John Franklin departed from the Thames with the *Erebus* and *Terror*, two more sturdy bomb vessels, in another search for the elusive North West passage. Their last contact with the outside world

was an encounter with the Hull whaleships *Prince of Wales* and *Enterprise* in Baffin Bay. Capt. Dannatt invited Franklin and several of his officers on board and he later reported the vessels fast to a large iceberg with a temporary observatory on the top of it. After that there was a total lack of news until 1850 when Capt. Ommaney of HMS *Assistance* found a scatter of naval stores and tinned food at Cape Riley, Devon Island. There were thirty-nine expeditions in search of the missing men and William Tather, a Hull whaling captain, was picked as sailing master of the *Investigator*, replacing Capt. Couldrey the original choice, in the 1848-49 expedition commanded by James Clark Ross.

Hull's direct involvement with whaling ended in 1869 but a number of the officers and men moved up to Scotland where fine new fleets of auxiliary steamers were sailing out of Dundee and Peterhead. Those that

*The sensational arrival in October 1833 of Sir John Ross aboard the Hull whaler **Isabella** (Capt. Humphreys) stimulated this dramatic presentation. It is interesting that the censor would not let the cast use Ross' name on stage, presumably because he was both a gentleman and a serving officer of the Royal Navy.*

THEATRE-ROYAL, HULL.

The new Drama, (produced for the first time on Friday Evening,) and received by a Crowded and highly Fashionable Audience with reiterated plaudits, will be repeated

This Evening, Tuesday, December 31st, 1833,
AND EVERY EVENING DURING THE WEEK, SATURDAY EXCEPTED.

In compliance with the mandate of the Vice Chamberlain, it will in future be performed under the title of

A VOYAGE
TO THE
NORTH!

Founded on the late Polar Expedition.

"Omit the name of Captain Ross throughout the piece. He may be called Captain only when directly spoken to, and the Captain of the Victory when mentioned.—Extract from the accompanying memorandum to License, by George Colman, Esq.

As this delicacy towards the illustrious Captain has been prescribed as the proper course, the Manager respectfully announces his submission and acquiescence.

The Overture, Vocal and Melo-Dramatic Music, composed, selected, and arranged, by Mr. IVERS.
The Scenery, (from authentic designs,) by Mr. TURNER and Assistants.
The Dresses by Mr. HOWELL, and Assistants.—Properties by Mr. & Mrs. SEYMOUR and Assistants.
The Machinery, &c. &c. by Mr. DIBBS and Mr. BAILES.

As the *interest* of Dramatic Representation, must be ever *heightened* by, if it does not *wholly* depend on, the introduction of the gentler sex; it has been necessary to interweave a *portion* of *fiction* with the adventures of the intrepid Voyager; these details have however been derived from an authentic story of a Dutch Captain, who was wrecked on a remote part of the Northern Coast—existed there four years—and was then restored to his country. Particular care has been taken not to *misrepresent* any events affecting the HERO OF THE DRAMA.

Act First.—Scene, London.—Time, May, 1829.
Act Second.—Embracing different portions of time in the Years, 1831 and 1832.—Scene, Arctic Regions.
Act Third.—Time, about Three Months previous to and inclusive of October 18th, 1833.
Scene, Arctic Regions, and Hull.

EUROPEANS.
Mr. Ransford, (a Merchant,)..................Mr. CHIPPENDALE.
Edward, his Nephew, (in love with Agnes,) ....Mr. EDMUNDS.
Lieut. Heartley, (in love with Rosabelle, *related* to the Captain of the Victory,)...Mr. W. L. REDE.
Mr. B. (a *friend* to the Captain.)...Mr. FAWCETT.—Clerk...Mr. SMITH—Bill Tulloch...Mr. HUMPHREYS.
Patrick O'Rourke, (a retired Veteran, half Sailor, half Gardener,)......Mr. DOWNE.
Mr. C. Thomas, (Ship Carpenter,).Mr HAMERTON.—Second Sailor.Mr.ANDREWS—Third Sailor.Mr.SMITH
Billy Bubble, (a Sojourner in the Metropolis, but late of Blanket-Row, Hull,) .....Mr. STANLEY
Servant to Mr. Ranford............Mr. SHOARD—Spectators at the departure of the Victory, &c. &c. &c.
Captain of the Victory................... ... .Mr. BASS.
Captain Fitzwalter, (having been Four Years domesticated with the Esquimaux,)......Mr. WALDRON.
Sailors, &c. Crew of the Victory.
Commander of the Isabella ...Mr. MADDOCKS.—Seaman......Mr. WATSON.—Second Sailor......Mr. JONES
Sailors, &c. Crew of the Isabella—Spectators, to welcome the gallant Captain to his Native Country.
Agnes Ransford, (a Young Lady all Sentiment and Song, daughter of Mr. Ransford,)..*Miss CAWSE.*
Rosabelle Rover Ransford, her cousin, a Young Lady *less* musically and *more* nautically inclined..Mrs.W. L. REDE.
Mrs. Farthingale, (Housekeeper to Mr. Ransford,)...........................Mrs.W. RUSSEL.
Emma Fitzwalter, (a Child aged Five Years,)...Miss SEYMOUR.
Mrs. Fitzwalter, (Wife of a Captain of a Whaling Ship, who is supposed to have been wrecked,)..Mrs. STANLEY

ESQUIMAUX.
Sbarouski } ...... Natives who have seen European Adventurers ..... { Mr HOWELL
Krieko } { Mr FAWCETT
Zawriekeus, (a Native who has *never* seen an European, *with a characteristic Melody*,) ... .Mr. DALE
Seal and Bear Hunters.........Messrs. Colville, Weedon, Brown, Havard, Shoard, &c.
Iligliuk, (" called by her Countrymen the Wise Woman," —see *Parry's Voyages*,) ....Miss WYNDHAM
Kafrauk, Ikookraw, Sgraeaw, Linhoo, &c......Mesdames Bass, Chippendale, Misses Fortescue, Stanley, &c.
Kagha, (an Old Woman, particularly referred to in the accounts of Captains Ross and Parry,)...Mr. SEYMOUR
Esquimaux Children.... ....Messrs. and Masters Seymour, &c. &c

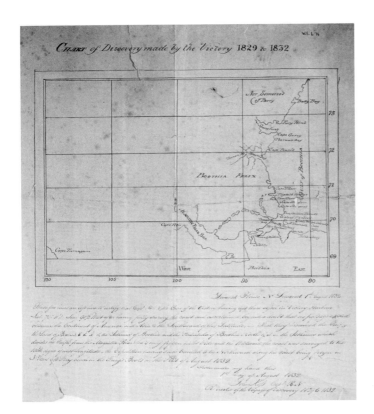

Chart of Discovery made by the Victory 1829 to 1832

Chart of discovery left by Sir John Ross at his base on Somerset Island, 1st August 1832 and later retrieved by Capt. Lee of the whaleship **Traveller***.*

Sir John Ross (1777-1856), Arctic explorer born at Inch, Wigtonshire. He made two attempts to discover the North West passage, in 1818 when in command of the **Isabella** *and in 1829-33 with the paddle steamer* **Victory***. British Consul at Stockholm 1839-45 and in 1850 led an expedition to search for Sir John Franklin.*

remained either transferred to the merchant trade or found a job ashore. William Wells, sometime master of the *Truelove*, made his last voyage north in 1867 and became the Haven Master at Hull. During this time he was consulted by Benjamin Leigh Smith, a gentleman explorer, who fitted out the *Sampson* which sailed from Hull in May 1870 to investigate the coast of Spitsbergen. The expedition reached 81° 24′N the farthest north of Spitsbergen since William Scoresby in 1806 and A. E. Nordenskiold who had pushed as far as 81° 42′ in 1848. The Spring of 1872 found *Sampson* fitting out in the tidal basin of Victoria Dock for another voyage amidst news that William Wells was to be appointed sailing master. In the event the position was filled by a William Blechynder but we do know that three former crewmen of the *Diana*, survivors of the terrible voyage of 1866-67, are recorded as being on board, Richard Byers, David Cobb and Magnus Nicholson a Shetland man. They had probably sailed in the previous year also, but no crew list has survived for that occasion.

Leigh Smith ordered a new vessel, the *Eira*, to be built to his own specifications at Peterhead under the watchful eye of David Gray, doyen of the Scottish whaling captains. A screw barkentine she set sail on 22 May with William Lofley as the ice master. Another survivor from the *Diana* it was he who had successfully navigated her back to Shetland in 1867 when there were only seven men fit enough to handle the rigging and the helm. He had then joined the Dundee whaling fleet as harpooner of the *Camperdown* under the command of Capt. John Gravill Jnr. son of his former master. Lofley hmself was master of the *Mazinthien* in 1871 and the *Nova Zembla*, 1876-77. During the outward voyage they met up with the whaleships *Hope* and *Eclipse*, captained by John and David Gray respectively. Lofley had his photograph taken on the decks of the *Eira* in a group which included Arthur Conan Doyle who had signed as surgeon of the *Hope*. Then an undergraduate from the medical school at Edinburgh University he

was to achieve lasting fame as the author of the Sherlock Holmes stories. The *Eira* cruised around the coast of Franz Josef land and one of the headlands on the south side of Alexandra land was named Cape Lofley, a name which is still marked on the charts though now in the Russian form of Mys Lofley. Leigh Smith's expedition was a great success and Lofley sailea as ice master of the *Eira* on a second voyage in 1881. This time the vessel received a severe nip not far from Cape Flora and sank, though thankfully there was time for a good quantity of provisions to be rescued. All twenty-five men successfully overwintered and they were rescued by a relief expedition which found them at Novaya Zemlya in August 1882 after they had made an epic open boat voyage. They covered four hundred and fifty miles in two walrus boats, each twenty feet long and furnished with sails made from table cloths, another testimony to Lofley's outstanding navigational skills. Richard Byers' son, George Robinson Byers, was with the 1881-82 party and was appointed as second mate. There were no more Arctic voyages for either man and Byers made his career in the merchant service with Hull's greatest steamship company, the Wilson Line.

Charles Edward Smith, surgeon of the *Diana* in 1866-67, made one more voyage to the Arctic. In 1869 he was persuaded by Sir Roderick Murchison of the Royal Geographical Society, who had heard of his exploits, to become surgeon and naturalist in an expedition with James Lamont, a Scottish gentleman. The vessel, a three-masted schooner, also named the *Diana*, sailed as far as Novaya Zemlya and visited Spitsbergen and Storfjord. There were however no significant scientific results and Lamont was more interested in finding interesting animals and birds to shoot than serious exploration.

In 1902 William Colbeck (1871-1930), chief officer of the ss *Montebello* of the Wilson Line in Hull, was chosen by the Royal Geographical Society to command the steam yacht *Morning* to convey stores and

Examples of the canned foods, prepared by Donkin and Gamble of Bermondsey, taken by Edward Parry on his 1823-25 expedition. The cache he left at Fury beach enabled Sir John Ross and his companions to survive four years marooned in the Arctic.

*Graffiti painted on the rocks at Cape Searle by Richard Byers when harpooner aboard the **Diana** in 1865. he died aged eighty-three on 4 February 1912, but this unexpected memorial remains visible to this day.*

*Capt. Lofley aboard the **Eira**, 1881, the bearded figure standing at the rear:*
from left to right Capt. David Gray, B. Leigh Smith, Dr. A. C. Doyle, Capt. J. Gray, Dr. Walker and Dr. Neale.

*Capt. Colbeck (on steps) and crew of the S.Y. **Morning***

*Bosun Alfred Cheetham posed with an ice anchor. A photograph taken by Herbert Ponting during Scott's **Terra Nova** expedition of 1910-13.*

*Llewellyn Wood Longstaff FRGS, FZS, chairman of Blundell Spence the Hull paint manufacturers, who personally financed Scott's **Discovery** expedition of 1901-04.*

chief magnetic observer in the British Antarctic Expedition of 1898-1900. Led by the Norwegian G. E. Borchgrevink they trekked as far as 78°50'S, at the time the most southerly point yet reached.

Gazetted sub-lieutenant Royal Navy Reserve Colbeck was now elevated to full lieutenant and proceeded with his vessel to Lyttelton in New Zealand before heading for the polar continent. Late in January 1903 the *Discovery* was sighted while Scott and his party were making their dash for the pole, reaching 82°17', further south than their predecessors. The Admiralty in the mean time had organised the Dundee whaler *Terra Nova* which was despatched post haste in support of the *Morning*, which they had taken responsibility for as well. Sailing from New Zealand again Colbeck found *Discovery* firmly stuck in the ice but she was blasted free with charges of guncotton buried in the ice and they all returned home to England. When Capt. Colbeck and nine of his crew arrived at Paragon Station in October 1904 they were welcomed by the Wilson Line prize band playing "Auld Lang Syne". Altogether eighteen Hull men had sailed to the Antarctic, ten of them from the crew of the ss *Montebello*. They included Rupert England, (second officer), Mr. Pepper, (midshipman), Alfred Cheetham, (bosun), Bibby, (carpenter), Burton, (sailmaker), Leary (Cook), Good, (bosun's mate), Leonard Burgess, Chester and Casement, (able seamen) and Kemp (fireman). Mr. R. Day was third officer of the *Terra Nova*. Capt. Colbeck in his calm relaxed way told reporters that his men had found time for recreation out on the polar ice, playing football and hockey. A *Hull* versus *Rovers* "derby" had been a notable event, using skis for goal posts and a bladder for a ball!

Scott named Cape Colbeck in his honour and the Colbeck Archipelago is named after his eldest son Capt. W. R. Colbeck who was surveyor in the British, Australian and New Zealand expedition of 1830-32 under Sir William Mawson.

It should also be recorded that the 1899-1904 British Antarctic Expedition led by Capt. Robert Falcon Scott

provisions to Captain Scott's Antarctic expedition. Educated at the Hull Grammar School and privately tutored by Zebedee Scaping, headmaster of the Trinity House Navigation School, he had previously been the

*Shackleton's **Quest** photographed on the Humber in July 1944,
when she was being used as a water carrier for the corvettes based at Immingham.*

was only made possible by the personal generosity of the sometime chairman of the Hull paint manufacturers, Blundell Spence. Llewellyn Wood Longstaff, colonel of the first volunteer battalion of the East Yorkshire regiment, was a great traveller and active on the council of the Royal Geographical Society. Following Sir Clements Markham's plea for funds Longstaff signed a cheque for £25,000, a princely sum for an individual benefaction of this kind. On 26 December 1902 during Scott's push southwards he named in his honour Mount Longstaff, a distinctive peak nearly ten thousand feet high, visible beyond the 83rd parallel.

Alfred Cheetham, bosun on the *Morning*, who served in the Wilson Line under Capt. Colbeck and Capt. Pepper claimed to have crossed the Antarctic circle no less than fourteen times. Born in Liverpool he settled in Bean Street and was subsequently to sail in Shackleton's expedition of 1907-09 in the *Nimrod* as third officer and bosun, with Scott in the *Terra Nova* as bosun, 1910-13, and again with Shackleton aboard *Endurance* as third officer in the 1914-16 Imperial Trans Antarctic Expedition. Cheetham received the polar medal and clasp and was lost when second officer of a minesweeper in the North Sea, torpedoed in 1918 just a few weeks before the end of the Great War.

Another Hull man on the *Endurance* was Charles Green who became known as the 'Antarctic chef'. He was with the party, which also included Cheetham, on Elephant Island when Shackleton made his epic open boat voyage to South Georgia to raise help. After climbing up the near vertical cliffs from the beach and crossing the rugged terrain of the island Shackleton and his companions finally reached the Norwegian whaling station at Grytviken.

Many Hull men served aboard the great whale factory ships operating in the South Atlantic. We might mention Frederick W. Jackson, J. G. Smith and J. Tye, all of whom were aboard the *Terje Viken* (United Whalers) immediately before the 1939-45 War.

After the end of hostilities Salvesens of Leith invested in the construction of a superb new whale factory ship named the *Southern Venturer*, 20,500 tons dead weight, and costing one and a quarter million pounds. She was launched in 1945 from the Smith's Dock yard at Middlesbrough and fitted with plant, for processing the meat into meal, by Rose Downs and Thompsons of Hull. On board to supervise the running of the new machinery was Mr. Robert Hewer to whom the trip was a magnificent adventure which he would never forget.

This summary of the activities of Hull men, and sometimes Hull ships, in the polar regions north and south shows a continuing connection with whaling and exploration spanning four hundred years. These voyages were driven by the desire for personal adventure, commercial gain and the urge to plant the national flag on new territory. Now that the globe is so extensively mapped not only by exploration on the ground, but by aerial and satellite survey too, the opportunities for blazing new trails are almost gone. The great goal for the future should be to truly comprehend our knowledge of the planet we live on and husband its resources to the benefit of all the peoples of the Earth.

APPENDICES

The Hull whaling trade falls into two distinct phases and the lists of vessels and their masters which follow have therefore been divided into two parts 1754-1842 and 1843-1869. No vessel was built uniquely for the whale fishery out of Hull, though many in the early nineteenth century were probably constructed with it in mind. It was common for vessels to pass in and out of the fishery depending on the current state of the oil and whalebone markets and the possibilities of getting a better return in the ordinary merchant trade. The majority of vessels were traders rendered suitable for whaling by the addition of extra planking on the hull and the provision of the necessary specialist gear. Only one British whaler was ever comprehensively designed and built for the Arctic fishery and that was the *Baffin* launched at Liverpool in 1820. She embodied the years of experience that her master and owner William Scoresby Jnr. had accumulated both in his own right and when sailing with his father. The *Baffin* started her career in a period when great success and high catches turned quickly to disaster and was wrecked at Greenland in 1830.

APPENDIX 1
THE HULL WHALING FLEET IN THE ARCTIC, 1754-1842

The earliest registration of some vessels in the port of Hull cannot be established since the first volume of the shipping register is missing. In such instances, e.g. *Adventure*, the earliest record is indicated as 'First reg. 1806', though she was certainly sailing out of Hull to the fishery in 1800. Where no entry is available, either because the vessel was lost before the second volume started in 1804, or because her registration details were never repeated in 1804 or afterwards (her owners remaining the same and the vessel being unaltered) the type of rig is uncertain unless a painting or other representation survives. In all other cases the vessel is ship rigged unless otherwise stated; tonnage is indicated immediately following, then period(s) in the whale fishery.

1. *ABRAM* (bark 306) 1819-41. Built Lancaster 1806. First reg. Hull 1819; to Kirkcaldy in 1855.

2. *ACTAEON* (   ) 1804-07.

3. *ADVENTURE* (336) 1800-04. From London. First reg. Hull 1806. Lost 1811.

4. *AJAX* (386) 1818. Built Hull 1802. First reg. Hull 1810; to Newcastle 1819.

5. *ALBION* (bark 1825; 323) 1811-23. Built Bridlington 1793. First reg. Hull 1810. Broken up, n.d. (after 1825). A namesake was in the Southern Fishery 1786-7.

6. *ALFRED* (322) 1810-21: 1825-35. Built Whitehaven 1796. First reg. Hull 1811; to Bo'ness, Linlithgow 1836.

7. *ALLIANCE* (428) 1787-93.

8. *ANDREW MARVEL* (377) 1812-36. Built Hull 1812. First reg. Hull 1812. Lost 1843.

9. *ANNA MARIA* (   ) 1799.

10. *ANN and ELIZABETH* (220) 1755-57: 1770-05. Lost at Orkney.

11. *ARIEL* (   ) 1799-1807: 1817-32. Lost at Davis Strait 1832.

12. *AUGUSTA* (386) 1811-14. Built South Shields 1800. First reg. Hull 1811. Lost n.d., after 1814.

13. *AURORA* (368) 1803-21. Built Selby 1782. First reg. Hull 1811. Lost at Davis Strait 1821.

14. *BATHIAH and MARY* (152) 1787-89.

15. *BENEDICTION* (177) 1787-90. Built Eddington, North Carolina, 1771. Lost at the fishery 1790.

16. *BENJAMIN I* (221) 1771-78.

17. *BENJAMIN II* (   ) 1782-88.

18. *BERRY* (315) 1754-75.

19. *BLENHEIM* (   ) 1797-1806. Captured n.d.

20. *BOSVILLE* (   ) 1755-56.

21. *BRITANNIA* (394) 1768-69: 1772-74. Lost at fishery 1774.

22. *BRITISH QUEEN* (350) 1767-75. Lost at fishery 1775.

23. *BROTHERS* (377) 1787-1809: 1811-20. Built Paull 1776. First reg. Hull 1805, lost 1820 at Davis Strait.

24. *BRUNSWICK* (357) 1814-34. Built Paull 1814. First reg. Hull 1814. Lost 1842 whilst trading.

25. *CAROLINE* (206). Built Salisbury, Mass. Bay, 1767. 1777-1800.

26. *CASTLE* (344) 1785-92.

27. *CATHARINE* (*sic*) (323) 1799: 1802-04: 1806:1809. Built Newcastle 1777. First reg. Hull 1805. Lost 1809 at Davis Strait.

28. *CATO* (bark 305) 1802-25. Built Newcastle 1783. First reg. 1804. To Lynn in 1828.

29. *CAVE* (   ) 1788.

30. *CERVANTES* (355) 1821. Built Greenock 1811. First

THEATRE-ROYAL, HULL.

On MONDAY Evening, January 5th, 1829,

His Majesty's Servants will perform Moore's Tragedy of THE

GAMESTER.

Beverley.	Mr CALVERT	Dawson.	Mr FISHER
Lewson.	Mr GARTON	Waiter	Mr T. KING
Stukeley.	Mr ANDERTON	Mrs. Beverley.	Miss DAVIES
Jarvis.	Mr DEARLOVE	Charlotte	Mrs FISHER
Bates.	Mr PHELPS	Lucy.	Miss YOUNG

After which, will be produced (for the third time) an entire new Pantomime, written and produced by Mr. W. L. REDE, called

HARLEQUIN HARPOONER;

Or, The Demon of the North Pole.

With new Local and Incidental Scenery, from drawings made for the occasion, and the latest discoveries, painted by Messrs. WILTON, W. REMINGTON, & DEARLOVE.—The Tricks, Properties, &c. by Mr. and Mrs. T. KING.—The Machinery by Messrs. YARNOLD, BAILES, and COLLISON.—The Dresses by Messrs. PERCIVAL, LAZENBY, and Assistants.—A new Overture composed by Mr. IVERS.

The entire of the Vocal and Pantomimic Music composed, selected, and adapted by Mr. CUMMINS.

Loskoff (a Norwegian Settler)	Mr WHITE
Slackhausen (his Servant)	Mr FISHER
Vondonderdronk (a Dutch Settler)	Mr DUFF
Huckaback (his Attendant)	Mr W. L. REDE
Tom Tulloch (the Harpooner)	Mr BAKER
Yackee (a genuine Uskee)	Mr W. KING
Demon of the North Pole	Mr ANDERTON
Sprite of Hecla	Master YARNOLD
Cecilia	Mrs FISHER
Syrens	Mrs. CUMMINS, Miss ANGELL, & Miss YOUNG.

Harlequin	Mr MATHEWS	Clown	Mr W. L. REDE
Pantaloon	Mr T. KING	Columbine	Mrs FISHER

The Characters in the Comic Scenes by the united strength of the Company.

Principal Vocal Performers.........Mrs. Cummins, Miss Angell, Miss Young, Miss Seymour, and Miss Andrews.—Messrs. White, G. Bennett, Young, Fisher, Dearlove, Hart, and Chorus.

Among the Incidental Scenery will be exhibited,

A SEA VIEW OFF THE ISLAND OF DISCO, ICE BERGS, &c. &c.
INTERIOR VIEWS OF SETTLERS HOUSES.—VIEW OF THE OCEAN.

Storm and Foundering of a Greenland Whale Ship.
INTERIOR VIEWS OF A VESSEL.

VIEWS OF HULL;

PIERS, AND MARKET-PLACE.

Temple Bar by Moonlight.

PAVILION OF THE SYREN.

With a variety of Tricks, Changes, and Transformations.

☞ Doors to be opened at Six, and the Performance to commence at Seven.

[No Orders can be admitted.]

T. Topping, Printer, Packet-Office, 51 Lowgate, Hull.

*Pages of the log of the **Abram** of Hull, 1839, Captain Couldrey. Very unusually a kill is indicatd by a full length drawing of a whale.*

The pantomime 'Harlequin harpooner' was evidently a burlesque of Arctic whaling and exploration probably at least in part inspired by the preparations being made by Captain Ross for another attempt to discover the North-West passage.

reg. Hull 1821; from Port Glasgow. Lost 1821 on only whaling voyage.

31. *CHANCE* (279) 1784-1800. Built Kent County, Maryland 1775.

32. *CHARLOTTE* (313) 1785-86.

33. *CHERUB* (   ) 1817-19. Built Liverpool 1814. First reg. Hull 1817 (from Belfast). Lost 1819 apparently after return from fishery.

34. *CICERO* (bark 1826; 325) 1819-26. Built Sutton (Hull) 1819. First reg. Hull 1819. Lost 1826 at Davis Strait.

35. *CLAPHAM* (374) 1813-15. Built Hull 1812. First reg. Hull 1812. Lost 1815, burnt at Greenland.

36. *COMET* (303) 1823-40. Built Rotherhithe 1791. First reg. Hull 1803. Lost 1843 whilst trading (1812-15 Southern Fishery).

37. *COUNTESS HOPETOWN* (sic) (   ) 1797-99. Lost at fishery 1799.

38. *COVE* (374) 1834-35. Built Whitby 1798. From Newcastle in 1834. Lost 1846 whilst trading (Relief ship in 1836).

39. *CUMBRIAN* (375) 1819-35. Built South Shields 1811. From Newcastle 1819. Lost 1844 whilst trading.

40. *CYRUS* (346) 1815-23. Built Sutton (Hull) 1815, Stephen and Son. First reg. Hull 1815. Lost 1823 at Greenland.

41. *DAUNTLESS* (261) 1829. Built 1818 Thomas Steemson, Hull. First reg. 1818. Lost 1829 at Davis Strait on only voyage to fishery.

42. *DIANA I* (331) 1785-94. Built Thorne 1784. First reg. Hull 1813. Lost 1817 whilst trading.

43. *DORDON* (286) 1820-35. Built Gainsborough 1820, Henry Smith. First reg. Hull 1820. Lost 20 October 1835 at Davis Strait.

44. *DUCKENFIELD HALL* (386) 1818-20. Built on Thames 1784. From London 1818. Broken up 1820.

45. *DUNCOMBE* (276) 1801-37: 1839. Built Thorne 1800. First reg. Hull 1807. To Stockton 1845.

46. *DWINA* (   ) 1802-04. Lost at fishery 1804.

47. *EAGLE* (289) 1813-33. Built Sutton 1813. First reg. Hull 1813, to Kings Lynn 1848.

48. *EARL FAUCONBERG* (   ) 1801-04. From Whitby. To Grimsby and lost 1821 at the fishery whilst on the Grimsby register.

49. *EBOR* (282) 1819-21. Built Hull 1815, Hall and Richardson. First reg. 1815. To London 1820.

50. *ECLIPSE* (283) 1817-19. Built Hull 1817, Hall and Richardson. First reg. 1817. To Aberdeen 1819.

51. *EGGINTON I* (304) 1787-1814 or 1815. (scrapped?).

52. *EGGINTON II* (336) 1815 or 1816-21. Built Paull, Thomas Steemson. First reg. 1815. To London 1824.

53. *ELIZA* (   ) 1803-04. Lost at fishery 1804.

54. *ELIZABETH* (322) 1784-1809: 1812-28. Lost 1828 at Davis Strait.

55. *ELIZABETH of SUTTON* (   ) 1788-90.

56. *ELLISON* (349) 1787-88: 1796-1839. Built Fishlake, Yorks 1777. First reg. Hull 1810. Lost 1846.

57. *EMPEROR* (327) 1802-07. Prize 1799. First reg. 1808. Condemned at Charleston n.d.

58. *ENDEAVOUR* (255) 1785-89. Lost at fishery 1789.

59. *ENTERPRISE* (   ) 1788-99. Lost at fishery 1799.

60. *EQUESTRIS* (393) 1810-19. Built Whitby 1795. First reg. Hull 1810. Lost 1819 at Davis Strait.

61. *EVERTHORPE* (bark before 1825; 349) 1810-11: 1813-37. Built Hull 1810. First reg. at Hull 1810. Lost 1839 whilst trading.

62. *EXMOUTH* (321) 1818-25. Built North Shields 1817. From Newcastle 1818; to Scarborough 1826.

63. *EXPERIMENT I* (237) 1810-11. Built William Henry, Lower Canada 1797. First reg. at Hull 1811. Lost 1832, whilst trading.

64. *EXPERIMENT II* (276) 1814-16. Built Baltimore, N. America 1763. First reg. 1814. Broken up 1817.

65. *FAME* (364) 1820-23. Prize 1795. First reg. Hull 1823; from Whitby. Lost 1823; burnt at Orkney.

66. *FANNY* (259) 1786-1804. Built Newbury, Mass. Bay 1772. Lost at fishery 1804.

67. *FREEDOM* (303) 1775-77: 1780.

68. *FRIENDS I* (256) 1787-90. Built Portsmouth, New Hampshire 1771.

69. *FRIENDSHIP* (410) 1813-21. Prize in 1808. First reg. 1813. Lost 1830 trading.

70. *GAINSBRO* (   ) 1788-91. Lost at fishery 1791.

71. *GARDINER and JOSEPH I* 1802-08. (Lost or scrapped?).

72. *GARDINER and JOSEPH II* (360) 1811-21. Built Sutton (Hull) 1810. First reg. Hull 1810. Lost 1824 whilst trading.

73. *GEORGE and MARY* (brigantine; 66) 1802-05. Built Wisbech 1801. First reg. at Hull 1814. Lost 1817 whilst trading.

74. *GIBRALTAR* (307) 1787-96. Captured.

75. *GILDER* (360) 1811-30. Built Paull 1811. First reg. Hull 1811. Lost 1830 at Davis Strait.

76. *GREENLAND* (310) 1778-79. Lost 1789 at the fishery. Appears on a painting of the Standidge fleet in 1789 and is probably the brig depicted thereon; Jackson gives a tonnage of 200.

77. *HANNIBAL* (316) 1818. Built West Stockwith, Notts. 1815. First reg. Hull 1815. To Aberdeen 1819.

78. *HARMONY I* (290) 1806-08: 1810-21: 1823-37. Prize 1799. First reg. at Hull 1804. To London 1853.

79. *HARMONY II* (380) 1821. Built at Lancaster 1798. First reg. Hull 1819. Lost 8 July 1821, on her only voyage to the fishery.

80. *HARMONY III* (364) 1830-32. Built Whitby 1809. First reg. Hull 1829. To Sydney in 1851.

81. *HEBE I* (365) 1820-21. Built Paull 1809. First reg. Hull 1820, from London. Lost 1821, on outward voyage.

82. *HENRY* (314) 1820-21. Built Sutton 1819. First reg. Hull 1819. Lost 1821 at the fishery.

83. *HIGH FLYER* (brigantine; 163) 1814-20. Prize 1813. First reg. Hull 1813. Lost 1820 at Greenland.

84. *HILLSTONE* (295) 1775-76: 1780.

85. *HOLDERNESS* (   ) 1802-06. Captured 1806.

86. *HOPE* (289) 1787-90. Built Boston, New England, 1785.

87. *HUMBER* (221) 1769-79. Lost at the fishery 1779.

88. *HUNTER* (247) 1799-1807. Built at Great Yarmouth 1787. First reg. Hull 1804. Lost 1807 at the fishery.

89. *INGRIA* (bark; 316) 1809-25: 1827-33. Built Whitby 1803. First reg. Hull 1809. Lost 1833 at Davis Strait.

90. *ISABELLA I* (91) 1786-87.

91. *ISABELLA II* (382) 1824-35. Built Hull 1813. First reg. Hull 1813. Lost 13 May 1835, at Davis Strait.

92. *JANE I* (   ) 1800. Lost on only voyage to fishery.

93. *JANE II* (330) 1809. Prize 1804. First reg. Hull 1809, from London. Broken up 1809.

94. *JANE III* (359) 1818-36: 1842. Built Hull 1813. First reg. Hull 1813. To Bo'ness, Scotland in 1847.

95. *JENNY* (   ) 1769-70.

96. *JOHN I* (   ) 1795-1802: 1804-05. Captured 1805.

97. *JOHN II* (343) 1810-21. Built Sutton (Hull) 1810. First reg. Hull 1810. Lost 1821 at the fishery.

98. *JOHN and MARY* (200) 1786-88.

99. *KIERO* (358) 1812-32. Built Hull 1811. First reg. 1811. Lost n.d., after 1834.

100. *KING OF PRUSSIA* (334 tons), 1771-75. Lost at the fishery 1775.

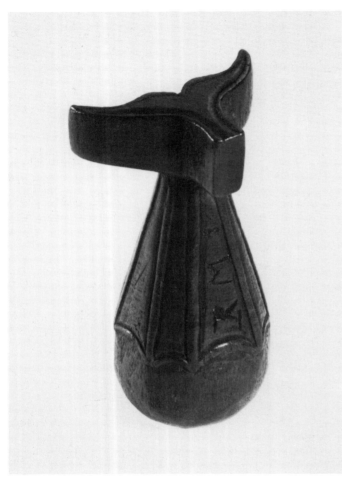

Stamp for making the mark of a whale's tail in the margin of the ship's log after a successful kill. It is carved with the initials of Robert Morley Sawyer (1816-1905) who sailed with his father, master of the **Harmony** *(I) in 1828 and 1829 while still a boy.*

Watch stand in the form of a miniature long-case clock. Made from oak it stands 13in high. The keyhole plate, balusters and lozenge decorations are neatly cut pieces of whale bone. It is dated 1835 the year in which its owner Capt. Henry Parish took command of the **Riby Grove**. *From 1831-34 he had been master of the* **Volunteer**, *a veteran of the Whitby fleet.*

101. *KINGSTON* (228) 1775-79.

102. *KIRKELLA* (bark; 409) 1821-22: 1829-31. Built Sculcoates 1814. First reg. Hull 1814. Lost 1837 whilst trading.

103. *KONIGSBERG* (254) 1810-11. Built Sutton 1804. First reg. Hull 1804. Lost 1811 at the fishery. Always listed in the customs registers as *Koningsberg*.

104. *LADY JANE* (340). 1788-1791.

105. *LAUREL I* (286) 1810-30. Built Peterhead 1801. First reg. at Hull 1809. Lost at the fishery 1830.

106. *LAUREL II* 1812-14.

107. *LEE* (363) 1813-35. Built Paull 1813. First reg. Hull 1813. Lost 1835 at Davis Strait.

108. *LEEDS INDUSTRY* (303) 1776-78.

109. *LEVIATHAN I* (   ) 1754-56: 1759-62: 1769.

110. *LEVIATHAN II* (410) 1803-21. Built 1803. First reg. Hull 1817. Lost at the fishery 1821.

111. *LONDON I* (   ) 1797-98.

112. *LONDON II* (273) 1814-17. Built Ipswich 1791. First reg. 1814. Lost with all hands 1817.

113. *LORD BARHAM* (321) 1813-18. Prize 1803. First reg. 1813 Sold n.d.

114. *LORD WELLINGTON* (354) 1811-21: 1824-34. Built Thorne 1810. First reg. Hull 1811. Lost 1834 at Davis Strait.

115. *LOTTERY* (334) 1799-1807. Condemned 1807.

116. *LYNX* (340) 1797-1811. Built Whitby 1776. First reg. Hull 1808. Captured n.d.

117. *MANCHESTER I* (266) 1770-1820. Built New York 1762. First reg. 1805. Broken up after 1820.

118. *MANCHESTER II* (285) 1806-24. Built West Stockwith, Notts, 1789. First reg. Hull 1806. Broken up 1827.

119. *MARGARET* (bark; 339) 1812-21. Built Montreal 1808. First reg. at Hull 1812. To Plymouth 1830.

120. *MARIA* (   ) 1794-1805. Lost at the fishery 1805.

121. *MARQUIS OF HUNTLY* (353) 1809. Prize 1804. First reg. Hull 1808. Lost n.d., whilst trading.

122. *MARY* (370) 1784-88.

123. *MARY AND ELIZABETH* (316) 1807-22. Built South Shields 1783. First reg. Hull 1807. Lost after 1824 whilst trading.

124. *MARY AND JANE* (   ) 1755-56.

125. *MARY OF SUTTON* (330) 1786-87. Lost at the fishery 1807.

126. *MARY FRANCES* (386) 1813-24: 1826: 1828-35. Built Hull 1783. First reg. Hull 1808. Lost 1835 at Davis Strait.

127. *MARY JANE* (   ) 1755-56.

128. *MERCURY* (bark; 346) 1820-27. Built Liverpool 1814. First reg. Hull 1819, from Liverpool. Lost 28 June, 1827, at Davis Strait.

129. *MINERVA* (234) 1788-93; 1795: 1797-99: 1801-08. Built Norfolk, Virginia 1765. First reg. 1809. To Newcastle 1833. Before 1797 voyages were apparently in the Southern Fishery.

130. *MOLLY* (291) 1775-1806. Built Boston, New England 1759. Captured 1806.

131. *MUNIFICENCE* (   ) 1802-08. Lost at the fishery 1808.

132. *NELLY* (278) 1804-07. Found abandoned 1797. First reg. Hull 1804. To London 1810.

133. *NEPTUNE* (329) 1816-23. Built Yarmouth 1809. First reg. at Hull 1814. Lost 1823 at Greenland.

134. *NORTH BRITON* (262) 1796-1830. Built Broad Oak, Gloucester, 1789. First reg. Hull 1805. Lost 1830 at Davis Strait.

135. *OAK HALL* (256) 1798-1809.

136. *OCEAN* (348) 1812-19. Built Yarmouth 1812. First reg. 1812. Lost 1819 at Davis Strait.

137. *OLIVE BRANCH* (   ) 1807. Lost on only whaling voyage.

138. *OXENHOPE* (bark; 286) 1829-30. Built Selby 1803. First reg. 1816. Lost 1830 at Davis Strait.

139. *PALLISER* (342) 1786-89. Built Carleby, Sweden 1779. First reg. Hull 1810.

140. *PERSEVERANCE* (bark 1825; 244) 1805-25. Built Hull 1784. First reg. Hull 1804. To Newcastle 1837.

141. *POOL* (   ) 1754-60.

142. *PRESCOT* (329) 1806-08: 1810-19. Prize 1794. First reg. Hull 1805. Broken up 1822.

143. *PRINCE OF BRAZIL* (237) 1810-16: 1818-20. Built Hull 1797. First reg. Hull 1810. To Newcastle 1822.

144. *PROGRESS I* (   ) 1805-07.

145. *PROGRESS II* (   ) 1818-30. Lost at fishery 1830.

146. *RACHEL AND ANN* (bark; 226) 1818-25. Built Hull 1800. First reg. Hull 1811. Lost 1826 whilst trading.

147. *RANGER* (309) 1786-89: 1791-92: 1794. Built Norfolk, Virginia 1775.

148. *RESOLUTION* (334) 1811-15. Prize 1808. First reg. Hull 1811. To London 1816.

149. *RIBY GROVE* (brigantine; 242) 1834-38. Built Whitby 1818. First reg. Hull 1818. Lost 1838 at Greenland.

150. *RICHARD* (304) 1808-19. Prize 1808. First reg. Hull 1808. Lost n.d.

151. *ROYAL GEORGE* (366) 1805-21. Built Newcastle 1793. First reg. Hull 1816. Lost 1826 whilst trading.

152. *ROYALIST* (428) 1812-14. Built Monkwearmouth 1793. First reg. Hull 1810. Lost 1814 at Davis Strait.

153. *SAMUEL* (244) 1785-1808. Built Saco, Mass. Bay 1774. Lost at the fishery 1808.

154. *SAMUELS* (398) 1803-08: 1810-19. Built at Whitby 1803. First reg. Hull 1805. Lost 1819, at Davis Strait.

155. *SARAH AND ELIZABETH* (270) 1784-1813; 1831-34. Built at Swan Creek, Maryland, North America 1775. First reg. Hull 1814. To London 1815. From London 1831. To London 1836 (Also sailed in the Southern Fishery *see* main text.)

156. *SCARTHINGWELL* (   ) 1788-96.

157. *SELBY* (199) 1787-94. Lost at fishery 1794.

158. *SHANNON* (350) 1814-21: 1831-32. Built Sutton (Hull) 1813. First reg. Hull 1814. Lost 1832 at the fishery.

(— *SIR HENRY MILDMAY* (   ) 1811 only listed by Capt. Barron.)

159. *SISTERS I* (303) 1813-17. Built Paull 1812. First reg. Hull 1813. To Kirkcaldy 1818. Lost at fishery 1819.

160. *SISTERS II* (bark before 1831; 308) 1831-37. Built Hull 1824. First reg. Hull 1824. To Sunderland 1852.

161. *SOUTHAMPTON* (345) 1772-73.

162. *SWAN* (320) 1815-19: 1823-40. Built Plymouth 1767. Sold out of the Royal Navy 1814. First reg. Hull 1815. To Aberdeen 1842 for breaking.

163. *SYMMETRY* (342) 1790-92: 1798-1821. Built Scarborough 1763. First reg. Hull 1815. Lost 1821 at the fishery.

164. *THOMAS I* (   ) 1802-08.

165. *THOMAS II* (355) 1810-22. Built Paull 1809. First reg. Hull 1809. To Dundee 1823 (lost at the fishery 1837).

166. *THORNTON* (262) 1803-06: 1809-21. Built Hull 1788. First reg. 1809. Lost 1821 at fishery.

167. *THREE BROTHERS* (357) 1812-15: 1817-18. Prize 1809. First reg. Hull 1809. Lost 1818 at Davis Strait.

168. *TRAFALGAR* (330) 1806-08: 1810-23. Built Gainsborough 1806. First reg. Hull 1806. Lost n.d.

169. *TRAVELLER* (   ) 1786-1807.

170. *TRITON* (434) 1774-78.

Plaque of whale jawbone showing the Right Whale hunt in the Arctic.
Note the characteristic double spout of the species
and the water draining from between the whalebone plates as it rises out of the water.

171. *TRUELOVE* (195: 293) 1784-89: 1796-1809: 1811-21: 1831-42. Built Philadelphia 1764. Captured from the American rebels. First reg. Hull 1810. To London 1874.

172. *UNITY* (bark: 270) 1818-23: 1825-26. Built Hylton Ferry, Durham, 1815. First reg. Hull 1818. Lost after 1827.

173. *VALENTINE* (245) 1809-10. Prize 1807. First reg. Hull 1809 from London. Lost 1810 apparently *after* returning from the fishery.

174. *VENERABLE* (bark 328) 1809-37. Built Scarborough 1798. First reg. at Hull 1809. Lost 1859.

175. *VESTAL* (   ) 1800-02.

176. *VOLUNTEER* (305) 1829-34. Built Whitby 1756. First reg. Hull 1829, from Whitby. Lost 1843, trading.

177. *WALKER* (335) 1807-24. Built Thorne, 1794. First reg. Hull 1806. Lost n.d.

178. *WHALE FISHER* (232) 1785-86. Lost 1786.

179. *WILLIAM* (bark 353) 1811-30. Built Sutton (Hull) 1811. First reg. Hull 1811. Lost 1830.

180. *WILLIAMSON* (   ) 1803-04.

181. *WILLIAM LEE* (367) 1831-36. Built Hull 1831. First reg. Hull 1831. Lost 1847, trading.

182. *WILLIAM TORR* (281) 1821-35. Built Hull 1821. First reg. Hull 1821. Lost 1835 at Davis Strait.

183. *YORK* (   ) 1754-57: 1759-60.

184. *YOUNG MARIA* (98) 1786-96.

185. *YOUNG RICHARD* (83) 1786-87.

186. *ZEPHYR* (342) 1810-37. Built Thorne 1796. First reg. Hull 1810. To London 1845.

30 vessels were built in Hull, or at least on the River Hull (the *Isabella* for example was almost certainly built at Beverley), inc. 9 at Sutton, 1 at Sculcoates and 8 at Paull. Also 1 at Selby and 5 at Thorne. On the East Coast: 8 at Whitby, 2 at Scarborough, 1 at Bridlington. Also 7 at Newcastle and Shields, 1 at Sunderland (Monkwearmouth), 1 at Hylton Ferry (also on the Wear) near Sunderland. South of the Humber in East Anglia, 6 at Gt. Yarmouth, 1 at Wisbech, 1 at Ipswich and 2 on the Thames. On the West Coast, 2 at Liverpool, 1 at Whitehaven and 2 at Lancaster.

2 were built at West Stockwith, Notts, 1 at Broad Oak, Gloucester and 1 (*Swan*) at the naval dockyard, Plymouth.

15 came from North America and 1 from Carleby in Sweden.

Like the *Swan* the *Adventure* may have been an ex-naval vessel. The *Truelove* included in the total of vessels from North America was a prize during the Revolutionary War. There were fourteen further prizes from the French wars. The remainder are of unknown origin.

APPENDIX 2
LOSSES OF VESSELS ENGAGED IN THE FISHERY 1754-1842

6 captured; 66 lost, plus 1 on Grimsby register and 2 after transfer to Scottish register, a total of 75. Five were lost on their sole excursion into the fishery.

ANN and ELIZABETH 1775 Lost at Orkney.

ARIEL 1832 at Davis Strait.

AURORA 1821. Lost at Davis Strait; crew saved.

BENEDICTION 1790.

BLENHEIM Captured by the enemy n.d. (when trading?).

BRITANNIA 1774.

BRITISH QUEEN 1775.

BROTHERS 1820 at Davis Strait; crew saved.

CATHARINE 1809 at Davis Strait.

CERVANTES 1821; crew saved.

CICERO 1826 at Davis Strait (New vessel 1819).

CLAPHAM 1815 burnt at Greenland (New vessel 1812).

COUNTESS HOPETOWN 1799.

CYRUS 1823 at Greenland (New vessel 1815).

DAUNTLESS 1829 at Davis Strait.

DORDON 1835 at Davis Strait 20th October (New vessel 1820).

DWINA 1804.

EARL FAUCONBERG 1821; lost from the Grimsby register.

ELIZA 1804.

ELIZABETH 1828 lost at the Davis Strait.

ENDEAVOUR 1789.

ENTERPRISE 1799.

EQUESTRIS 1819 lost at Davis Strait; crew saved.

FAME 1823 burnt at Orkney *en route* to the fishery.

FANNY 1804.

GAINSBRO 1791.

GIBRALTAR 1796. Captured by the French.

GILDER 1830 lost at Davis Strait.

GREENLAND 1789.

HARMONY (II) 1821 crew saved.

HEBE (I) 1821 lost on outward passage.

HENRY 1821 crew saved (New vessel 1819).

HIGH FLYER 1820 at Greenland, crew saved.

* *HOLDERNESS* 1806 Captured.

HUMBER 1779.

HUNTER 1807.

INGRIA 1833 at Davis Strait, (New vessel 1803).

ISABELLA (II) 1835; lost 13 May at Davis Strait.

JANE (I) 1800 lost.

JOHN (I) 1805 Captured by enemy.

JOHN (II) 1821; crew saved (New vessel 1810).

KING OF PRUSSIA 1775.

KONIGSBERG 1811.

LAUREL (I) 1830 at Davis Strait.

LEE 1835 at Davis Strait (New vessel 1813).

LEVIATHAN (II) 1821; crew saved (New vessel 1803).

LONDON (II) 1817 at Davis Strait with all hands.

LORD WELLINGTON 1834 at Davis Strait (New vessel 1810).

LYNX captured n.d. (when trading ?).

MARIA 1805.

In his retirement William Barron gave a number of illustrated lectures on the whaling trade and published his book 'Old Whaling Days' in 1895.

BETHEL
United Methodist Church,
CHARLOTTE STREET, HULL.

On MONDAY, Dec. 16th,

CAPT. BARRON

WILL DELIVER HIS POPULAR

 **LECTURE**

ENTITLED:

OLD WHALING DAYS

Life in the Arctic Seas.

A large number of Slides will be exhibited by a Powerful Electric Lantern.

(Mr. NORMAN ASHTON, Prospect Street, Hull, Lanternist.)

An interesting Lecture on experiences about which there is a great fascination. For Seventeen years Capt. Barron saw neither ripening corn, growing flowers, blossoms nor fruit on the trees; whilst his constant surroundings were ice, snow, fogs, or the boundless expanse of ocean. The Lecture has a great charm for all, old or young for the adventures so graphically described are all true.

The Lecture will be interspersed with Solos.

Chairman, Mr. J. W. DUNCAN.

A SILVER COLLECTION.

Doors open at 7 o'clock.
Commence at 7-30 prompt.

*Wage return of William Barron in 1864 as mate of the Dundee whaler ss **Polynia** under Capt. Gravill Snr. For nearly seven months at sea he earned just over £80 which after deductions for purchases from the ship's stores and the allowance (allotment) paid to his family he was left with a balance of £37.4s.6d.*

(F)   **ACCOUNT OF WAGES.**

SANCTIONED BY THE
BOARD OF TRADE,
FEBRUARY 1864.

Name of Ship and Official Number.	Name of Master.	Description of Voyage or Employment.
S.S. "Polynia"	John Gravill	Seal and Whale Fishing

Name of Seaman.	Date of Engagement.	Date of Discharge.	Rate of Wages.
Wm. Barron	24 Feb/64	13 Sep/64	55/- p month

Wages :—	Amount.			Deductions.	Amount.		
for 6 months 21 days 55/- p month	18	8	6	Advance	10	2	,,
Hand money	7	7	,,	Allotment	16	10	,,
Seal Oil money on 120 Tons @ 8d p Ton	48	,,	,,	Fines and Forfeitures	,,	4	,,
				Cash to a/ in May	22	,,	,,
Seals Skins money on 11.100 Skins @ 3/- pr 100	16	13	,,	do ,, a/ 16 & 17 Sep	2	2	,,
				Extra Stores	,,	19	2
				Capt a/	1	7	10
	90	8	6	Shipping Fees	,,	3	,,
Deductions as p contra	53	4	,,				
Balance due .... £	37	4	6	Total Deductions .... £	53	4	,,

Dated at the Port of _Dundee_

this _19th_ day of _Sept_ 18_64_

for John Gravill by Batchelor

Signature of Master.

NOTICE TO MASTERS.—One of these Accounts must be filled up and delivered to each Member of the Crew at least Twenty-four Hours before he is paid off, under a penalty not exceeding £5, and no Deduction will be allowed unless duly inserted.

[*Turn over.*

LONDON ; Printed by GEORGE E. EYRE and WILLIAM SPOTTISWOODE, Printers to the Queen's most Excellent Majesty.

*William Blythe commanded the **Brunswick** (Wright Bowden and Wright) from her maiden voyage in 1814 to 1834, the vessel's last season in the Arctic. He was highly successful, averaging fourteen whales a season, and died in his eighty-eighth year on 13 September 1870, at his home in Wright Street.*

MARY FRANCES 1835 at Davis Strait.

MARY OF SUTTON lost at fishery 1787.

MERCURY 1827 at Davis Strait.

*MOLLY 1806 captured.

MUNIFICENCE 1808.

NEPTUNE 1823 at Greenland; crew saved.

NORTH BRITON 1830 at Davis Strait.

OCEAN 1819 at Davis Strait; crew saved (New vessel 1812).

OLIVE BRANCH 1807.

OXENHOPE 1830 at Davis Strait.

PROGRESS (II) 1839.

RIBY GROVE 1838 at Greenland.

ROYALIST 1814 at Davis Strait.

SAMUEL 1808.

SAMUELS 1819 at Davis Strait (New vessel 1803).

SELBY 1794.

SHANNON 1832 at Davis Strait (New vessel 1813).

SISTERS (I) lost from Kirkcaldy register, 1819; (New vessel 1813).

SYMMETRY 1832; crew saved.

THOMAS (II) lost from Dundee register, 1837; (New vessel 1809).

THORNTON 1821; crew saved.

THREE BROTHERS 1818 at Davis Strait.

WHALE FISHER 1786.

WILLIAM 1830 at Davis Strait (New vessel 1811).

WILLIAM TORR 1835 at Davis Strait; with all hands (New vessel 1821).

New vessel indicates recently built at the time of introduction in the whale fishery; the actual date of construction is indicated where known.

Though Grimsby was later to be Hull's great rival in the trawling industry only two ships were entered in the whale fishery, the *Earl Fauconberg* (ex Hull and Whitby) lost in Davis Strait 1821 and the *Birnie* lost in 1813, also at Davis Strait.

Page of the log of the **Truelove** *1859, Captain William Wells, Thomas Hunter mate.*

Barque Truelove in Davies' Straits

Week Day	Winds	
Thursday April 28th	S E	AM commences with light breeze and fine clear weather at Noon Saw a fish Sent 2 Boats on the watch at 1.30 PM Thomas Goodwill Shot a fish at 6 P. took her along side at 9 commenced to flince. Latter part
	S S E	light breeze and fine clear weather Served out to the crew 62 Pound of Beef
Friday April 29	S E	AM light breeze all hand employed Flincing at 6 P. set the watch Ship plying up towards Whale fish Islands. Midle and latter part D. weather Ship plying as above on the lookout for whales 5 Sail in Sight
	E S E	Served out to the crew 26 Pound of Pork and fish
Saturday April 30th	S E	AM throughout these 24 howers light breeze and fine clear weather at 6 AM called all hands to make off the fish blubber at 10 PM Set the watch Ship running of to the west in Sarch of Whales to the end
		Served out to the crew 31 Pound of Beef and 26 of Pork
Sunday May 1st	S E	AM fore and middle light airs and fine clear weather at 10 D. Saw Several fish at the Pack edge at 3 PM George Wright and William Heywood boat Shot at 1 fish together at 5 D. died at 6 D. took

*George Lister master of the Thornton 1814-18. He was mate of the **Shannon** under the command of his kinsman George Davey when she was lost at Davis Strait, 26 April 1832. Lister is recorded as dock master in 1851 when he was aged sixty-three.*

Whalebone (baleen) cribbage board decorated with simple scratch designs of ships.

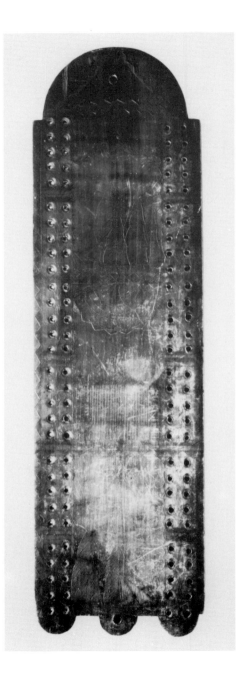

ADAIR, James 1812-17 *Manchester* (I);

ALLAN or ALLEN, James 1785-6 *Whale Fisher*; 1792: 1794-5 *Egginton* (I); 1797-1801 *Ellison*.

ALLAN or ALLEN, John 1811 *Manchester* (I); 1815-25 *North Briton*.

ANDERSON, J. 1760 *Pool*.

ANGUS, James 1820-1 *Gardiner and Joseph* (II).

APPLETON, Robert (master of *Adventure* 1806 and possibly during her whaling career 1800-4).

ARMSTRONG, 1798: 1801 *Traveller*.

ASH, Robert 1818 *John* (II); 1819-20 *Manchester* (II); 1821-6 *Everthorpe* 1827-37 *Zephyr*.

BANKS, 1797-8 *Lynx*.

BARCHARD, John 1818-19 (*William*).

BARRY, 1803 *Samuel*.

BEADLING, William 1811-14 *Augusta*; 1812-21 *Cyrus*.

BEAUTYMAN, 1795 *Elizabeth*; 1797 *Countess Hopetown*.

BELL, Edward 1810-15 *Zephyr*; 1818-19 *Unity*.

BENNETT, John 1812-31 *Venerable*; 1832 *Kiero*; 1833: 1835 *Ellison*.

BENNETT, Robert 1819-20 *Thornton*.

BLENKINSOP, 1802-4 *Munificence; 1806-8 Oakhall*; 1810-11 *Laurel*.

BLENKINSOP, 1810-13 *Laurel* (I).

BLENKINSOP, Joseph 1814-20 *High Flyer*.

BLYTH, William 1814-16: 1818-34 *Brunswick*.

BOWLEY, (or Bourley), Robert, 1815: 1817 *Friendship*.

BOWSER 1812-13 *Equestris*.

BOYDON or BOYDEN, John 1821 *Lord Wellington*.

BRAMHAM, John 1827-8 *Elizabeth*; 1829 *Dauntless*; 1830-1 *Harmony* (III).

BRASS, William 1817-22 *Thomas*; 1823-4 *Comet*; 1825-29 *Eagle*; 1830-5 *Alfred*; 1836 *Ellison*.

BREWIS, William 1817-24 *Eagle*.

BRIGGS, John 1803-8 *North Briton*; 1810-11 *Samuels*.

BRIGGS, 1811 *Lynx*.

BROWN, 1789 *Alliance*.

BRUCE, George 1812-17 *Brothers*; 1818-26 *Gilder*.

BURRELL, Robert (see also Bowley) 1807 *Minerva*; 1813-14 *Friendship*.

BUSER 1795 *Caroline*. (See *Bowser*).

BUTLER, R 1758 *Pool*.

BUTTERY, 1815-17 *Elizabeth*.

CAMP, John 1798 *John*.

CARLILE or CARLILL, John 1829-30 *Kirkella*.

CARLILL, Robert 1835 *Isabella* (II).

CARTER, John 1821 *Thornton*.

CHADWICK, William 1835 *Cove*.

CHESTER, John 1831-3 *Eagle*.

CLARK, Robert 1777 *Kingston*; 1784-94: 1796-8 *Truelove*.

CLARK, William 1820-1 *Alfred*.

CLARK(E), 1807 *Prescott*; 1810-14 *Symmetry*; 1815-20 *Laurel* (I).

CLOUGHTON, 1806 *Prescott*; 1808 *Symmetry*.

COLLEY, 1798-1801: 1803-4 *Oakhall*; 1806-7 *Ariel*.

COLQUHOUN, James 1818-20 *Elizabeth*; 1821-9 *Kiero*.

COOK, Thomas 1814 *Experiment* (II); 1815-19 *Mary and Elizabeth*.

CORBETT, John 1820-22 *Duncombe*.

COULDREY, William Stanley 1823-4 *Duncombe*; 1825-7 *Mercury*; 1828-35 *Mary Frances*; 1839-40 *Abram*.

COUSINS (COUZENS: COZENS or COUSEN), Samuel 1815-19 *Ocean*; 1820-1 *Hebe* (I); 1822-3 *Abram*; 1824 *Mercury*.

CREIGHTON, James 1818-20 *Rachel and Ann*; 1821 *Margaret*; 1825 *Rachel and Ann*.

CRIGHTON, 1802 *North Briton*.

CROMPTON, Thomas 1804-7 *Nelly*; 1809-10 *Thornton*; 1811-12 *Prescot*; 1813-15 *Lee*; 1816-19 *Prescot*.

DANNATT, Edward 1814-20 *Trafalgar*; 1821-25 *Laurel* (I); 1826-30 *Progress*; 1831-4: 1836 *Sisters* (II).

DANNATT, Philip 1811-14 *Mary and Elizabeth*; 1815-20 *Lord Wellington*; 1821-34 *William Torr*.

DAVIDSON, James 1754-5 *Pool*; 1757 *Ann and Elizabeth*.

DAVY (or DAVEY), George 1832 *Shannon*.

DEAN, Joseph 1835 *Sisters* (II); 1836-7 *Duncombe*; 1838 *Riby Grove*; 1839 *Duncombe*.

DICK, 1803 *Egginton* (II) 1804-8 *Elizabeth* [probably John Dick, as following].

DICK, John 1810-15 *Alfred*; 1816-18 *Mary Frances*.

DOBBYN, Peter 1771: 1775 *Berry*.

DRING, Henry 1773-4 *Benjamin*.

DRING. Robert 1815-19 *Duncombe*; 1823-40 *Swan* (I).

DRING, Robert Jnr. 1833-5 *Cumbrian*.

DRIVER, Thomas 1810 *Konigsberg*.

DUNCAN, T 1768 *Britannia*.

EDINGTON, 1811 *Sir Henry Mildmay* (only listed by Barron).

EDMONDS, 1803 *Brothers* [probably same master as follows].

EDMONDS, Anthony 1797-8 *London*; 1801 *North Briton*; 1804-10 *Brothers*; 1812-14 *Royalist*.

ELSEY, Henry 1814 *Three Brothers*.

EWBANK, 1803-9 *Sarah and Elizabeth*.

EZARD, John 1811 *Resolution*.

FARROW (FARRAR), George 1816-17 *Lord Barham*; 1818-19 *Manchester* (I).

FISHER, Andrew 1754-7 *York*; 1773 *Humber*.

FOORD, Humphrey 1770: 1777 *Manchester*.

FOSTER, 1802-4 *Emperor; 1806-7 Traveller*.

FOSTER, 1804-10 *Royal George* (probably same person as following).

FORSTER (or FOSTER), Thomas 1811 *Truelove*; 1821-6 *Lee*.

GAMBLIN, Stephen 1821 *Jane* (II).

GASCOIN(E), Robert 1809 *Elizabeth*; 1814-17 *Margaret*.

GAWTHORPE, James 1814-17 *William*; 1818-20 *Progress*.

GEE, John 1777-8 *Caroline*.

GIBSON, 1803-4 *Adventure*; 1805 *Progress*.

GILYOTT, William 1817-19 *Richard*; 1820-1 *Dordon*.

GLENTON, William 1819-20 *Kiero*; 1820 *Harmony* (II).

GOFF, John 1755 *Mary and Jane*.

GREEN, George 1821 *Friendship*.

GREEN, John 1788: 1792-3: 1795: 1798 *Scarthingwell*.

GREENSHAW, 1799-1803 *Truelove*; 1804 *Williamson*; 1805: 1811 *Royal George*.

GREENSHAW, John 1754-5 *Leviathan*; 1757 *Pool*.

GRIME, 1809 *Richard*.

GRISWOOD, Matthew 1818-19 *Hunter*.

GROAT, Walter 1801-5 *Hunter*; 1806 *Symmetry*.

HALL, Ed. 1788: 1791 *Molly*.

HALLER, 1809-10 *Manchester* (I).

HARPER, 1812-14 *Laurel* (II).

HARRISON, Richard 1811-24 *Walker*; 1825-34 *Lord Wellington*.

HARRISON, William 1819-21 *Abram*.

HAWKINS, Thomas 1810-11 *Ellison*; 1813-15 *Everthorpe*; 1816-17 *Leviathan*; 1818-19 *Everthorpe*; 1820-27 *William*.

HEDON (or HEADON), George 1825 *Andrew Marvel*.

HEWITT, James 1798: 1801-2 *Sarah and Elizabeth*; 1803-4 *North Briton*; 1806-7 *Progress*; 1808 *Elizabeth*; 1809 *Symmetry*; 1812-3 *Margaret*.

HIBBS, John 1833-8 *Abram*.

HILL, Richard 1831-2 *William Lee*.

HOLBERRY, 1806-9 *Ellison*.

HOLBERRY, John 1803-4 *Samuel*; 1805 *Egginton*; 1811-16 *Gardiner and Joseph* (II).

HOLBERRY, Thomas 1810-11 *Richard*; 1818-19 *Margaret*.

HORD, Jeremiah 1784 *Mary*.

HORNBY, 1801 *Duncombe*.

HORTON, 1811 *William*.

HUMPHREY, Richard Wallis 1820-3 *Albion*; 1824-5: 1827-30 *Isabella*; 1831 *Kirkella*; 1832-4 *Isabella*. Ice master of relief vessel *Cove*, 1836.

HUNTER, Archibald 1806: 1809-14 *Manchester* (II).

HUNTER, James 1807-13 *Perseverance*.

HURD, 1814 *Elizabeth*.

HURST, William 1812-16 *Richard*; 1817-23 *Ariel*.

HUTCHINSON, 1789 *Samuel*.

JACKSON, Samuel 1830-2 *Ellison*.

JACKSON, William 1817-19 *Cherub*; 1820-3 *Mercury*; 1824-32 *Abram*.

JAMESON, Andrew 1802-4 *Cato*.

JAMESON, Peter 1811-14 *North Briton*.

JENNINGS, 1803 *Fanny*.

JENNISON, 1801-2 *Fanny*; 1803 *Egginton*.

JOHNSON, 1812 *Lord Wellington*.

JOHNSTON(E), John 1819-24 *Ellison*; 1825-6 *Alfred*; 1827-37 *Everthorpe*.

JOHNS(T)ON, John 1819-25 *Cumbrian*; 1826 *Unity*.

JUBB, J 1792 *Diana* (I).

JUBB(S), John 1804-6 *Thornton*.

KEARSLEY, 1810-3 *Sarah and Elizabeth*.

KELAH (or KEILAH), Robert 1804 *Truelove*; 1805-8 *Manchester* (I); 1809-11 *Venerable*; 1812-13 *William*; 1814-21 *Shannon*.

KINSLEY, 1811 *Sarah and Elizabeth*.

KIRBY, Thomas 1811 *Konigsberg*; 1812-14 *Ellison*; 1815 *Leviathan*; 1816 *Egginton* (II); 1817-19 *Gardiner and Joseph* (II).

KITCHINGMAN, Charles 1815 *Ellison*; 1816 *Everthorpe*; 1817 *Egginton* (II); 1818-21 *Leviathan*; 1822-5 *Cato*.

KNIGHT, William 1828-9 *Comet*.

KNILL, Thomas 1813: 1818-19 *Ingria*; 1821 *Symmetry*; 1822 *Mary and Elizabeth*; [1814-17 *Ingria* Neal; no doubt the same person].

LAMBERT, J 1812-14 *Lord Wellington*.

LANKESTER (or LANCASTER), George 1823-4 *Manchester* (II).

LAZENBY, Samuel 1777-8 *Humber*.

LEAF, William 1821-2 *Cicero*.

LEAKE, 1812-13 *Three Brothers*.

LEE, Thomas 1819-21 *Ebor*; 1822 *Manchester* (II); 1823-6 *Cicero*; 1827-35 *Lee*; 1836 *William Lee*; 1837-9 *Ellison*.

LEWIS, Benjamin 1814-16 *Equestris*.

LINSKILL, William 1824-30 *Dordon*; 1831 *Ariel*.

LISTER, George 1814-18 *Thornton*.

LLOYD, William 1821-3 *Trafalgar*.

MCBRIDE, 1798: 1801-4 *Minerva*.

MCBRIDE, Peter 1810-18 *Harmony* (II); 1819-20 *Friendship*.

MCINTOSH, James 1820-5 *Ingria*; 1829-30 *Oxenhope*.

MCKENZIE, George 1832-6 *Venerable*; 1837 *Sisters* (II).

MCKENZIE, James 1826 *Isabella* (II); 1827-30 *Gilder*; 1831 *Isabella*.

MCKIVER, 1801-4 *Maria*.

MABB, William 1788 *Brothers*.

MADDISON, Josiah 1815-18 *Three Brothers*; 1819-20 *Duckenfield Hall*; 1821 *Cervantes*; 1822-32 *Jane* (II).

MALLARD, John 1755 *Bosville*.

MANGER, William 1815-20 *Symmetry*; 1823-5 *Progress*; 1827-30 *Laurel* (I); 1831-7 *Truelove*.

MARKHAM, John 1829-30 *Volunteer*; 1831 *Comet*.

MARSHALL, John 1795: 1797-8: 1801 *Brothers*; 1804: 1806-7 *Samuels*; 1810-11 *John*.

MARSHALL, 1803 *Samuels*.

MARSHALL, Richard 1813-14 *Sisters* (I); 1815-17 *John* (II); 1818 *Hannibal*; 1820 *Margaret*; 1821-22 *Rachel and Ann*.

MARSHALL, Thomas Harrison 1810-14 *John* (II); 1815-16 *Thomas* (II).

MARTIN, John 1824-6 *Elizabeth; 1827-9 Alfred*; 1830-1 *Kiero*; 1832-7 *Comet*.

MATSON, F 1795-6: 1798: 1800-4 *Manchester* (I).

MATTHEWS, William 1814-17 *London*.

MAXWELL, P 1797 *Blenheim*; 1798 *Countess Hopetown*.

MERCER, Matthew 1818-20 *Brothers*; 1821-2 *Progress* (II).

MILNER, William 1804-9 *Truelove*; 1810 *Prince of Brazil*.

MITCHESON, 1803 *John* (I).

MITCHESON, 1803 *Dwina*.

MITCHINSON, William Henry 1798 *Blenheim*; 1801 *John*; 1803 *Dwina*; 1809 *Marquis of Huntly*.

MITCHISON, John 1810-11 *Prescot*; 1812 *Experiment* (I); 1813 *Thornton*; 1821 *Manchester* (II).

MORRIS, Martin 1813-15 *Mary Frances*; 1816-19 *Alfred*.

MUGG, Richard 1795 *Samuel*; 1798 *North Briton*; 1803 *Catharine*.

MUNROE, Martin 1813-15 *Clapham*; 1816-23 *Neptune*; 1824-5 *Exmouth*; 1826-32 *Cumbrian*.

MURRAY, James 1817-18 *Manchester* (II).

NEAL (see Knill), 1814-17 *Ingria*.

NESBITT (or NISBETT), William 1814-16 *Perseverance*.

NEWHAM, 1795, *Molly*.

NEWHAM, Nathaniel 1819-21 *John* (II); 1823-4 *Rachel and Anne*; 1825-7 *Comet*.

NICHOLSON, Andrew 1754 *Berry*.

NICHOLSON, 1803-5 *Lottery*.

NORTH, Thomas 1828-30 *William*.

ORTON, Thomas 1810 *Duncombe*; 1811 *William*; 1812-24 *Andrew Marvel*; 1825-6 *Perseverance*; 1829-30 *Andrew Marvel*.

OVERTON, Thomas 1812-15 *Royal George*; 1817-19 *Equestris*.

PAGE, 1803-5 *Holderness*.

PALMER, 1801-2 *Lynx*.

PARISH, Henry 1831-4 *Volunteer*; 1835-37 *Riby Grove*.

PARKER, 1802-3: 1805 *Ariel*.

PARKER, John Snr. 1830-2 *Harmony* (I); 1833-5 *William Lee*; 1838-42 *Truelove*.

PARKIN, William 1818 *Lord Barham*; 1819-20 *Cicero*.

PATTISON, 1817-9 *Perseverance*.

PATTISON, John 1755 *Ann and Elizabeth*; 1759-61 *Leviathan*.

PEARSON, Isaish 1813-15 *Lord Barham*.

PECKET, Joseph (see Picket).

PHILIPS, 1813 *Resolution*.

PICKERING, 1814 *Egginton* (I).

PICKET, Joseph 1815 *Experiment* (II); 1816-21 *Royal George*.

PIERPOINT, Richard 1813-14 *Eagle*.

PINKNEY, Robert 1810-15 *Egginton* (I); 1816 *Ellison*.

PLAXTON, James 1809-1810 *North Briton*; 1811: 1814-19 *Samuels*; 1820-2 *Henry*.

POTTS, John 1779 *Molly*.

PRESCOTT, 1811 *Brothers*.

RHOADES, Thomas 1820 *Everthorpe*; 1821-3 *Elizabeth*.

RIPON, 1805 *Samuel*.

ROBINSON, James 1833-4 *Jane*.

ROGERS, 1827-30 *Ariel*.

ROSE, Hunter 1794-5 *Sarah and Elizabeth*; 1798: 1801-5 *Symmetry*; 1806 *Hunter*; 1807-8 *Trafalgar*; 1809 *Jane* (I); 1810 *Trafalgar*; 1811 *Lord Wellington*.

ROSE, John 1795-8 *Enterprise*; 1801-2 *Lottery*; 1803 *Eliza*; 1804-7 *Actaeon*; 1809-10 *Valentine*; 1815-17 *Sisters* (I).

ROSS, 1806 *Catharine*.

SADLER, Angus 1796-9: 1801-2 *Molly*; 1803-17 *Aurora*.

SADLER, Joseph 1802 *Dwina*; 1804-5 *Molly*; 1807-11 *Walker*; 1811-14: 1816-17 *Gilder*; 1818-20 *Jane* (II).

SADLER, Peter 1784: 1788-9: 1792-4 *Manchester* (I).

SAWYER, Charles 1823-9 *Harmony* (I).

SAWYER, Morley 1819-21 *Harmony* (I).

SCOFFIN, William 1825-35 *Duncombe*.

SCORESBY, William Snr. 1820-3 *Fame*; Vessel on Hull register 1823 only.

SHORT, William 1820-3 *Unity*.

SILCOCK, George 1826-8 *Andrew Marvel*.

SINCLAIR, Charles 1788 *Enterprise*.

SLATER, Samuel 1832 *Dordon*.

SLINGSBY, John 1818-19 *Albion*.

SMART, 1817 *Albion*.

SMITH, Joseph Anderson 1802-3 *Earl Fauconberg*.

SNAITH, George 1835 *William Torr*.

SOFTLEY, George 1825 *Unity*.

SOMERVILLE, Andrew 1831 *Sarah and Elizabeth*.

SPENCE, Thomas 1825-29 *Ellison*.

STANDIDGE, Samuel 1767 *British Queen* [other seasons too, dates uncertain].

STEPHENS, John 1818 *Ajax*.

STEWARD, 1789 *Resolution*.

STOREY, James 1826-30 *North Briton*; 1831 *Shannon*.

STORRY, 1802 *Egginton* (I); 1803 *Elizabeth*; 1804: 1806-7 *Gardiner and Joseph* (I).

STORY, John 1817-18 *Ellison*.

TATE, 1805-7 *Munificence*.

TATHER, 1798 *Elizabeth*.

TATHER, John 1797-8 *Elizabeth*; 1804: 1806-14 *Leviathan*; 1817 *Everthorpe*; 1818 *Egginton* (II).

TATHER, William 1823-4 *Sarah and Elizabeth*; 1835-6: 1842 *Jane* (II).

TAYLOR, John 1810-14 *Thomas*; 1815-16 *Swan* (I).

TAYLOR, Joseph 1805-14 *Duncombe*; 1817-19 *Swan* (I); 1820 *Manchester* (I).

TAYLOR, Robert 1792: 1796-1798 *Fanny*.

TAYLOR, 1811-2 *Prince of Brazil*.

THOMAS, Joseph 1816 *Experiment* (II); 1817-19 *Eclipse*; 1820-1 *Aurora*; 1822-3 *Dordon*.

THOMAS, W 1755-68 *Berry*.

THOMPSON, Edward 1817 *Brunswick*; 1818-23 *Exmouth*.

THOMPSON, George 1833-6 *Harmony* (I).

THOMPSON, P 1755 *Molly*.

THOMPSON, Robert 1822 *Perseverance*.

TREADGOLD, 1807 *Emperor*.

TODD, Thomas 1813-16: 1818-20 *Prince of Brazil*; 1821 *Truelove*.

TRUEMAN, Rickinson 1806-9 *Egginton* (I); 1810-11 *Everthorpe*; 1812-18 *Kiero*.

TURNBULL, Andrew 1817-21 *Cato*; 1823-4 *Perseverance*.

TURPIN, Ephraim 1818 *Duckenfield Hall*.

UNTHANK, John 1815 *Gilder*; 1816-26 *Zephyr*.

VENNIS, 1802-3 *Traveller*.

WAKE, 1806 *Lottery*; 1808 *Richard*; 1811-12 *Trafalgar*.

WAKE, Robert 1809-11 *Mary and Elizabeth*.

WALLACE, 1803-4: 1806-7 *Lynx*.

WALLIS, 1795 *Minerva*.

WARD, Isaac 1837 *Venerable*; 1838-40 *Comet*; 1841 *Abram*.

WARD, Samuel 1812-14 *Elizabeth*; 1815-16 *Manchester* (II).

WATSON, Henry 1812-20 *Truelove*; 1821 *Kirkella*; 1824-6 *Ariel*.

WEBSTER, 1798 *Samuel*; 1801-2 *Samuel*; 1803-4 *Thomas* (II).

WEBSTER, Alexander 1809-11 *Ingria*; 1812-14 *Ocean*.

WELBURN, 1801 *Samuel*; 1804 *Blenheim*.

WELBURN, John 1815-16 *Eagle*.

WELBURN, Matthew 1820-1 *Perseverance*; 1822-3 *Cyrus*.

WHELDON, Henry 1820 *Mary and Elizabeth*.

WILDEN, John 1805-16 *Cato*.

WILDEN (or WILDON), Turner 1809-10 *Lynx*; 1811-16 *Albion*.

WILKINSON, 1795: 1797-8 *Maria*; 1801 *Ariel*; 1802 *George and Mary*.

WILLBY, 1803 *Blenheim*.

WILLIAMS, Robert 1821 *Mary and Elizabeth*.

WILLIAMSON, Joseph 1812 *Thornton*; 1813-15 *Prescott*; 1816-20 *Lee*.

WILLIS, Edward 1831 *Dordon*; 1832 *Ariel*; 1833-5 *Dordon*; 1837 *Harmony* (I).

WILSON, 1803 *George and Mary*.

WILSON, 1827-33 *Ingria*.

WILSON, Gower 1834 *Riby Grove*.

WILSON, Henry 1834 *Ellison*.

WILSON, John 1814-15 *Resolution*; 1819-21 *Egginton* (II).

WILSON, Mark 1795: 1798 *Caroline*; 1796 *Manchester* (I).

WILSON, William 1834 *Cove*.

WOODHALL, Charles 1830 *Comet*.

WOOD, R 1792 *Selby*.

WOODS, 1802 *Adventure*; 1803 *Duncombe*.

WRAY, William 1798: 1793-5 *Gibraltar*; 1798: 1801 *Egginton* (I); 1803-4 *Ellison*; 1807-9 *Mary and Elizabeth*.

WRIGHT, Matthew 1830 *Eagle*; 1831-6 *Andrew Marvel*.

YOUNG, 1809 *Catharine*; 1810-11 *Egginton* (I).

YOUNG, George 1810-11 *Equestris*.

APPENDIX 4
HULL WHALING FLEET 1843-69.

There were a total of 38 vessels in the fleet during this period, slightly more than a third of which were lost at the fishery. Those marked with an asterisk were sailing in the fishery at some time prior to 1842.

Only three vessels were built locally (Hull, Goole and Scarborough), four on the Thames, three in the North East, two in Lancashire, two in Scotland and two in Devon. Six were constructed in Canada, three in the USA and three on the continent. A single vessel originated in Calcutta, another two are simply listed as foreign and two were prizes.

The fleet was very heterogeneous with a variety of rigs from smack to ship. Steam was first introduced in 1857 in the *Diana*. A total of eight steam vessels sailed in the fishery, for each of which the gross tonnage is indicated. The most vessels to sail in a single season was fifteen in 1846.

(1)* *ABRAM* (bark; 319) (1819-41) 1844-53, to Kirkcaldy 1855.

187. *AEOLUS* (ship; 394) 1858-65 foreign built; unknown. First reg. Hull 1853: lost 1865 at the Fishery.

188. *ANNE* (brig; 254) 1844-55: 1857-61. Bt. Sunderland 1832; first reg. Hull 1844, from Newcastle. Lost 1861 at the Fishery.

189. *ARGO* (brig; 111) 1850. Bt. Prince Edward Island 1842. First reg. Hull 1850, from Newfoundland. To N. Shields 1859.

190. *BON ACCORD* (ship; 365) 1844-7. Bt. Blythe, Northumberland 1812. First reg. Hull, 1844, from Aberdeen. Wrecked 1847 at the fishery.

191. *CHASE* (steamship; 559) 1858-60. Bt. Medford, Mass. First reg. Hull 1858, from London. Lost 1860 at the fishery.

192. *CONSTANTIA* (brig; 113) 1843-6. Prize 1809. First reg. Hull 1841, from London. Lost n.d.

193. *CORKSCREW* (steam schooner; 160) 1859. Blackwell 1844. First reg. Hull 1854; from Goole. Sold abroad 1862.

194. *DIANA (II)* (steamship; 355) 1856-69. Bt. Bremen 1840. First reg. Hull 1856. Aux. steam engine installed 1857. Lost 1869 homeward bound.

195. *ELIZA* (brig; 142) 1846-50. Bt. Hampton, New Brunswick 1834. First reg. Hull 1845, from London. To London c.1850?

196. *EMMA* (bark; 379) 1855-62. Bt. Calcutta 1809. First reg. Hull 1855; from London. To Dundee 1863.

197. *EMMELINE* (steam schooner; 504) 1859. Bt. Hull 1856. First reg. Hull 1856. To Liverpool 1859 [lengthened 1848: 622 tons gross].

198. *FLAMINGO* (brig; 185) 1851-3. Bt. Aberdeen. To Folkestone 1854.

199. *FORTH* (schooner; 151) 1843-7. Bt. Borrowstoness (Bo'ness), Linlithgow 1831. First reg. Hull 1842 from Borrowstoness. Lost 1847 (after return from fishery?).

200. *FRIENDS (II)* (schooner; 42) 1848. Bt. Hull 1808. First reg. Hull 1843, from Wisbech. To Whitby 1850.

201. *GERMANICA* (brig; 203) 1851-4. Bt. Gröhn, Hanover n.d. First reg. Hull 1850. Lost 1854 at the fishery.

202. *GERTRUDE* (steambark; 569) 1859. Bt. 1855. First reg. Hull 1861, from Grimsby. Reg. at Grimsby for whaling career.

203. *HEBE* (brig; 140) 1844-54 (II). Bt. Goole, Ralph Atkinson 1834. First reg. Hull 1834. Lost 1854 at the fishery

204. *ISABEL* (steam brigantine; 138) 1859-60. Bt. St. Peters, Prince Edwards Island. First reg. Hull 1858, from London. To London 1861.

(94)* *JANE (II)* (ship; 359) (1818-36: 1842) 1843-6. First reg. Hull 1813. To Bo'ness 1847.

205. *LABUAN* (steam barque; 589) 1859. Bt. Liverpool 1855. First reg. Hull 1859, from Liverpool. Lost 1864. (Lengthened 1860: 899 tons gross).

206. *LADY SEALE* (steam schooner; 184) 1860-3. Bt. Dartmouth 1846. First reg. Hull 1853, from Exeter. On London reg. for whaling. Wrecked 1863 at fishery.

207. *LORD GAMBIER* (ship; 407) 1845-52. Bt. Monkwearmouth 1825. First reg. Hull 1845, from Newcastle. To Kirkcaldy 1853.

208. *ORION* (brig; 235) 1852-4. Bt. Finland ca. 1840. First reg. Hull 1851. Lost n.d.

209. *PLEDGE* (smack; 30) 1849. Bt. Sandwich, Kent 1846. First reg. Hull 1848; from Ramsgate. Wrecked 1849 at the fishery.

210. *PRINCE OF WALES* (ship; 352) 1844-9. Bt. Rotherhithe 1793. First reg. Hull 1844; from London. Lost 1849 at the fishery.

211. *ROSE* 1851-3. Grimsby registered.

212. *RUFUS* (brig; 110) 1851-2. Prize; reg. London 1847. First reg. Hull 1850. Lost 1855.

213. *ST. GEORGE* ( ) 1846-54. London registered.

(155)* *SARAH and ELIZABETH* (barque; 268) 1844-9: 1851-7. Bt. Swan Creek, Maryland 1775. Reg. Hull 1843 from London. Lost 1857 at the fishery. (Also served in the Southern fishery; see main text).

214. *SWALLOW* (ketch; 158) 1845-9. Bt. Cross Park, Devon, 1827. First reg. Hull 1845 from London. Lost 1849 at the fishery.

215. *SWAN (II)* (brigantine; 95) 1850-3: 1855-6: 1858-62. Bt. Harbour Breton, Newfoundland 1830. First reg. 1850; from London. To London 1865.

(171)* *TRUELOVE* (bark; 296) 1843-63: 1866-8.

216. *TURK* (sloop; 31) 1848-9. Bt. Plymouth 1842. First reg. Hull 1845, from Plymouth. Lost n.d.

(174)* *VENERABLE* (bark; 328) (1809-37) 1852-3: 1855. First reg. Hull 1809. Lost while trading 1859.

217. *VIOLET* (brig; 191) 1853-4. Foreign built, no details. First reg. Hull 1853. Lost 1854 at the fishery.

218. *WILDFIRE* (ship; 406) 1859. Bt. Quebec 1854. First reg. Hull 1856. To Dundee 1860.

219. *WILLIAM WARD* (ship; 296) 1846-9, Built Pugwash, Nova Scotia 1837. First reg. Hull 1838, from Halifax, Nova Scotia. Wrecked 1849 at the fishery.

Of the entire fleet of over 200 vessels 65% of the total sailed in the fishery for five years or less, indeed 30% of the total entered the fishery for only one season, 20% served between 6 and 10 years, 12% for 11-20 years and 3% for 21 years and over. The *Truelove* served a total of 72 seasons, between 1784 and 1868 with several periods of general trading during this span of service. Outstanding is the *Manchester*, which served for 51 years without a break, before being broken up in 1827. The *Molly* sailed 32 seasons without a break and the *North Briton* 35 seasons. The *Duncombe* sailed for 38 seasons to the Arctic with one season off to break the sequence, the *Brothers* sailed 33 seasons, with a two year gap and the old *Harmony* for 30 seasons, with two seasons off. 56% of all the vessels sailed to the fishery without intermission.

The *Sarah and Elizabeth* served a total of 47 seasons in the Arctic between 1784 and 1857 when she was lost. In between she was a trader and also spent some six years in the South Sea fishery.

APPENDIX 5
LOSSES AT THE FISHERY 1843-1869.

Total of 15 vessels lost:-

AEOLUS 1865 at coast of Iceland 3 May (Greenland).

ANNE 1861 at Davis Strait.

BON ACCORD 1847 at Davis Strait 4 July.

CHASE 1860 at Davis Strait.

DIANA 1869 at Donna Nook; (from Davis Strait).

GERMANICA 1854, 19th June, at Greenland.

HEBE 1854, 21 May.

LADY SEALE (London registered) 1863 at Davis Strait.

PLEDGE 1849.

PRINCE OF WALES 1849 at Davis Strait.

ROSE 1853 at Davis Strait.

SARAH and ELIZABETH, 1857: 12 April at Greenland.

SWALLOW 1849, 3 June.

VIOLET 1854 at Greenland.

WILLIAM WARD 1849 at Greenland.

Seven of these were lost the same season when a new master was appointed. The *Pledge* made only the one voyage.

WHALING MASTERS 1843-69.

BARRON, William 1861 *Truelove*.

BIRCH, William 1852-4 *Germanica*; 1855 *Venerable*.

BROWN, William 1844-5 *Jane* (II); 1846-7 *Eliza*; 1848 *Friends* (II); 1849 *Turk*.

BUSHBY, 1858-9 *Swan* (II).

BUSHBY, Richard 1846-7 *Forth*; 1852 *Rose*.

CAWCUTT, William 1851-4 *Hebe* (II).

COLQUHOUN, Joseph 1849 *Pledge*.

COULDREY, 1853 *Rose*.

COULDREY, Thomas 1852 *Swan* (II); 1854 *Violet*.

COULDREY, William Stanley 1844 *Prince of Wales*; 1845-7 *Abram*; 1850-52 *Lord Gambier*.

DANNATT, Edward 1845 *Prince of Wales*.

DAY, Robert. April 1868 only, *Diana* (II).

DEAN, Joseph 1843 *Constantia*; 1844-7 *Anne*.

FELL, Thomas 1851 *Sarah and Elizabeth*.

GALE, William 1853 *Swan* (II).

GOOD, John 1848 *Abram*.

GRAHAM, John 1848-50 *Eliza*; 1851 *Germanica*.

GRAVILL, John 1844-5 *Constantia*; 1846-9 *William Ward*; 1849 (Franklin search); 1850-3 *Abram*; 1854-5 *Sarah and Elizabeth*; 1856-7 *Diana* (II); 1858-60 *Chase*; 1861 *Diana* (II); [1862-4 *Polynia of Dundee*]; 1865-6 *Diana* (II).

GRAVILL, John Jnr. 1856-7 *Sarah and Elizabeth*; 1858-60 *Diana* (II).

GRAY, (Joseph or John) 1860-5 *Aeolus*.

GROAT, Henry 1843 *Forth*; 1845-50 *Hebe* (II).

HIBBS, John 1858-9 *Aeolus*.

HILL, Richard 1848-9 *Lord Gambier*.

HUMPHREYS, Richard Wallis 1844 *Abram*.

HUNTER, Thomas 1846 *Constantia*; 1848-9 *Anne*.

JACKSON, William 1845 *Lord Gambier*; 1853 *Violet*.

LEE, Thomas 1844-7 *Bon Accord*; 1849 *Prince of Wales*.

LEE, Thomas Jnr. 1845 *Swallow*; 1846-8 *Prince of Wales*; 1849 *Swallow*; 1851-3 *Flamingo*.

LEETHAM, William 1859 *Corkscrew*.

LOWDEN, Samuel 1848 *Swallow*.

MARTIN 1852-3 *Venerable*.

NICHOLSON, Robert 1845 *Forth*; 1846 *Jane* (II); 1850 *Swan* (II).

PARISH, Henry 1843 *Jane* (II).

PARKER, John 1843-53 *Truelove*; 1854-5: 1857-8 *Anne*; 1860 *Truelove*.

PARKER, John Jnr. 1855-8 *Emma*; 1860-1 *Lady Seale*.

PATTERSON, John 1846-7 *Lord Gambier*.

PEACE, Jonathan 1846 *Swallow*.

PINKNEY, William 1851-2 *Rufus*.

ROBINSON, 1860-1 *Swan*.

SILVEY, John 1861 *Anne*; 1862 *Lady Seale*; 1868 *Diana* (II).

SIMPSON, George 1859-60 *Isabel*; 1862 *Diana* (II).

SKINNER, William 1858 *Turk*; 1850 *Argo*.

TATHER or TETHER, Richard 1859-60 *Anne*.

THORNHAM 1859 *Wildfire*.

TOOGOOD, James 1844 *Forth*.

WALKER, 1863: 1868 *Truelove*.

WELLS, Emanuel 1847 *Swallow*; 1852-4 *Orion*.

WELLS, Richard 1862 *Truelove*; 1862 *Lady Seale*; 1869 *Diana* (II).

WELLS, William 1844-5 *Hebe* (II); 1846-9 *St. George*; 1850-3 *Anne*; 1854-59 *Truelove*; 1861-2 *Emma*; 1863 *Diana* (II); 1866-7 *Truelove* [*Narwhal*, Dundee in 1864].

WILLIS, William 1844-9: 1852-3 *Sarah and Elizabeth*; 1855-6 *Swan* (II).

WILSON, John 1859 *Labuan*.

Of the grand total of over three hundred whaling masters 40% served in the fishery for five years or less (30% of the total for only one season), 19% for six to ten years, 13% for eleven to twenty years and 2% for twenty or more years. There were five men who were master for twenty years, namely Robert Ash, William Blyth (the whole of this time in command of the *Brunswick*), William Brass, William Manger and Martin Munroe. A further seven were master for *more* than twenty years including the brothers Philip and Edward Dannatt, twenty-four and twenty-three years respectively, Richard Harrison for twenty-four years, W. S. Couldrey for twenty-two years. John Parker Snr. served for no less than twenty-seven years, closely followed by Thomas Lee with twenty-six years of command.

More than half, 59% were master of only one vessel throughout their career, 25% only two vessels, 9% three vessels and 5% commanded four ships. Of the remaining 2% four masters served in six vessels, two had seven vessels and one, Thomas Lee Snr. a total of eight ships between the years 1819 and 1849. John Gravill commanded six vessels in the Hull fleet and the *Polynia* of Dundee.

PRIZE VESSELS AND TRANSFERS FROM THE ROYAL NAVY

Ship *ADVENTURE*: Ex navy? Purchased from Government by former owners. Built at Whitby at unknown date. Registered London 30 April 1795. Transferred to Hull 31 March 1806.

Ship *EMPEROR*: Prize to HMS *Astrea*. Formerly called *Leifde*. Condemned as a prize 13 November 1798 and made free by certificate 18 February 1799. Registered Hull 18 May 1808.

Ship *FAME*: William Scoresby Snr's. ship. She was apparently built at Goa, the Portuguese colony, on the west coast of India, in either 1734 or 1738. Called *Fame* when taken from Portuguese by French Sloop of war *Marseilles*. Taken from French by HMS frigate *Blanche*. Sold by order of court of Vice Admiralty at Rosean, Dominica, 18 June 1794. Duty paid at Liverpool 9 February 1795. Certificate of registry granted at Whitby 19th March 1819. Transferred to Hull 4 April 1823. A contemporary model showing her construction is in the Hull Trinity House.

Ship *FRIENDSHIP*: Prize made free by judges certificate 23 January 1808; registered in Hull 1 March, 1813.

Ship *HARMONY*: Taken by the private vessel *Lark*, Capt. Henry Tucker, 7 May 1799; and condemned as a prize in Court of Vice Admiralty of New Providence, 17th July 1799. Made free by certificate granted at London 28 July 1800. Registered in Hull 18 March 1804.

Brigantine *HIGH FLYER*: Prize made free by judges certificate 10 February 1813. Detained at Hull by the substitute to the marshal of the Admiralty prior to hostilities against the USA. Condemned as a lawful prize by judges certificate 10 February 1813. Registered in Hull 19 April 1813.

Ship *JANE* (II): Prize to HMS *Cyanne* and condemned at Antigua 14 January 1804. Made free at Bristol 24 December 1804; register granted at London 4 February 1807. Registered at Hull 23 February 1809.

Ship *LORD BARHAM*: Prize made free by judges certificate 11 October 1803. Registered at Hull 20 January 1813.

Ship *MARQUIS OF HUNTLY*: Prize formerly called *Jan Frederick*; taken prior to hostilities with the Batavian Republic. Condemned and made free by certificate dated 16 May 1804. Registered at Hull 12 November 1808.

Ship *NELLY*: Found aground and abandoned at Meynean Island, St. Vincent, March 1797 by Capt. Brown of HMS *Beaver*. Sold by order of the judge of the Vice Admiralty to pay salvage and other expenses and for the benefit of those who might appear entitled to the nett proceeds. Supposed formerly to have belonged to Liverpool. This is recorded by the register granted at Kingston, St. Vincent, 15 May 1797; the vessel having been captured by the enemy and condemned was sold to a neutral and since purchased by a British subject. Registered at Hull 8 March 1804.

Ship *PRESCOT*: Captured by the fleet under Sir John Jarvis and legally condemned in the court of Admiralty at Guadeloupe 4 July 1794. Made free by certificate granted at London 24 September 1795. Registered at Newcastle 26 January 1803 and transferred to Hull 16 March 1805.

Ship *RESOLUTION*: Prize made free by judges certificate 22 January 1808. Registered at Hull 23 March 1811.

Ship *RICHARD*: Taken prior to hostilities with Denmark. Judges certificate granted 15 January 1808 and made free 1 March 1808. Registered in Hull 30 March 1808.

Ship *SWAN*: Built at HM yard, Plymouth, and launched 21 November 1767. As recorded in the certificate granted 29 November 1814. Registered in Hull 19 January 1815. This vessel featured in the Nore mutiny.

Ship *THREE BROTHERS*: Prize made free by judges certificate 22 June 1808. Registered in Hull 20 October 1809.

Ship *TRUELOVE*: Built at Philadelphia in 1764 and captured during the American War of Independence.

Ship *VALENTINE*: Prize taken by HMS *Amiable*. Condemned at Martinique 20 April 1798. Distressed at London 21 July 1799. Taken by French in May 1807 and recaptured and condemned as a prize at Jamaica. Registered at Kingston, Jamaica, 12 September 1807. Entered on the London registry 1 August 1808. Transferred to Hull 28 February 1809.

Post 1842 fleet:

Brig *CONSTANTIA*: Foreign built and formerly called the *Doris* she was taken as a prize and legally condemned at the High Court of Admiralty, 11 February 1808. Made free 20 February 1809 and registered 23 February at London in the same year. She sailed in the Hull whaling fleet 1841-6 and was lost at an undetermined date.

Brig *RUFUS*: Condemned in British and Brazilian Court of mixed Commission at Sierra Leone for breach of laws made for the prevention of the slave trade. Registered at London 5 March 1847 and transferred to Hull 1850. Lost in 1855.

APPENDIX 8
VOYAGES OF THE *TRUELOVE* 1784-1868

Date	Destination	Departure and Arrival	Master	Whales caught	Bone	Oil (tons)
1784	Greenland	16 March — 26 July	R. Clark	—	approx. 42 cwts.	32
1785	Greenland	1 March — 3 August	R. Clark	—	46 cwts.	16
1786	Greenland	19 March — 2 August	R. Clark	—	47 cwts.	46
1787	Greenland	20 March — 12 July	R. Clark	4 (13 seals)	4 tons	72
1788	Greenland	—	R. Clark	3	2 tons	41½
1789	Greenland	—	R. Clark	4 (1 bear, 2 seals)	2½ tons	51
1790	Greenland	—	R. Clark	1 (1700 seals)	2 cwts.	29
1791	Greenland	—	R. Clark	1 (27 seals)	15 cwts.	16
1792	Greenland	—	R. Clark	4 (17 seals)	3 tons	52
1793	Greenland	—	R. Clark	1	1 ton	50
1794	Greenland	—	R. Clark	1	—	23
1795	Oporto trade	—	Stephenson	—	—	—
1796	Greenland	11 March — ?	R. Clark	3	3 tons	60
1797	Greenland	4 March — 21 July	R. Clark	11	4½ tons	90
1798	Greenland	—	R. Clark	6	—	43
1799	Greenland	returned 17 July	Greenshaw	14 (97 seals) (3 unicorns)	—	101
1800	Greenland	returned 29 July	Greenshaw	10 (37 seals)	3¼ tons	65
1801	Greenland	—	Greenshaw	14	3 tons	96½
1802	Greenland	—	Greenshaw	6	4½ tons	83
1803	Greenland	returned 22 July	Greenshaw	4 (60 seals)	2½ tons	66
1804	Greenland	returned 1 August	W. Milner	4 (1800 seals)	2 tons	52
1805	Greenland	returned 23 July	W. Milner	9	3 tons	103
1806	Davis Strait	returned 29 July	W. Milner	8	—	120
1807	Davis Strait	returned 21 August	W. Milner	2	—	39
1808	Greenland Seas	returned 5 August	W. Milner	19 (210 seals)	—	105
1809	Greenland	—	Milner	12	—	111
1810	Oporto trade	—	T. Foster	—	—	—
1811	Davis Strait	—	T. Foster	9	—	124
1812	Davis Strait	28 Feb — 28 August	H. Watson	14	—	158
1813	Davis Strait	—	H. Watson	1	—	22
1814	Davis Strait	—	H. Watson	12	7 tons	165
1815	Davis Strait	—	H. Watson	8	5 tons 7 cwt.	105
1816	Davis Strait	—	H. Watson	10	8 tons	138
1817	Davis Strait	—	H. Watson	6	—	92

Date	Destination	Departure and Arrival	Master	Whales caught	Bone	Oil (tons)
1818	Davis Strait	—	H. Watson	7	—	93
1819	Davis Strait	—	H. Watson	7	—	83
1820	Davis Strait	—	H. Watson	14	—	180
1821	Greenland	—	Todd	3	—	54

1822 — 1830 TRADING

Date	Destination	Departure and Arrival	Master	Whales caught	Bone	Oil (tons)
1831	Davis Strait	(A bethel ship)	W. Manger	3	2½ tons	40
1832	Davis Strait	—	W. Manger	28	8 tons	174
1833	Davis Strait	—	W. Manger	22	9 tons	150
1834	Davis Strait	—	W. Manger	9	3 tons	80
1835	Davis Strait	returned 28 October	W. Manger	shared a whale with another ship	10 cwt.	15
1836	Davis Strait	returned 24 October	W. Manger	1	10 cwt.	9
1837	Davis Strait	returned 4 August	W. Manger	1 (26 seals)	5 cwt.	5
1838	Davis Strait	—	J. Parker	16	5 tons 16 cwt.	100
1839	Davis Strait	—	J. Parker	9	7½ tons	112
1840	Davis Strait	—	J. Parker	2	1½ tons	28
1841	Davis Strait	—	J. Parker	4	1½ tons	28
1842	Greenland	—	J. Parker	(1620 seals)	—	19
1843	Davis Strait	25 March — 26 September	J. Parker	12½*	7½ tons	130
1844	Davis Strait	16 March — 25 November	J. Parker	5	3½ tons	70
1845	Davis Strait	29 March — 6 October	J. Parker	32	7 tons	130
1846	Davis Strait	28 March — 24 November	J. Parker	—	1¼ tons	20
1847	Davis Strait	17 March — 15 November	J. Parker	16	5 tons	85
1848	Davis Strait	25 March — 11 November	J. Parker	—	3¾ tons	74
1849	Davis Strait	31 March — 6 October	J. Parker	—	9 tons	160
1850	Davis Strait	6 April — 2 November	J. Parker	3	2 tons	40
1851	Davis Strait	5 March — 30 October	J. Parker	5	4 tons	75
1852	Davis Strait	24 March — 11 November	J. Parker	? — and 500 seals)	2 tons (64 bundles of whale fins)	94 tons
1853	Davis Strait	returned 25 October	J. Parker	9	105 cwt.	95
1854	Davis Strait	10 March — 24 October	W. Wells	—	2½ tons	42
1855	Davis Strait	7 March — 20 October	W. Wells	2	1 ton	19
1856	Davis Strait	20 February — 26 October	W. Wells	11 (2 live bears) (7 dead bears)	6 tons	110
1857	Greenland	2 March — 28 July	W. Wells	? — and 342 seals)	12 cwt.	117

* 18 casks of bottlenose whale blubber taken in at Shetland — refers to 1843 voyage above.

Date	Destination	Departure and Arrival	Master	Whales caught	Bone	Oil (tons)
1858	Davis Strait	27 February — 30 October	W. Wells	? — (2 polar bears)	4 tons	70
1859	Davis Strait	15 March — 23 October	W. Wells	—	6 tons	100
1860	Davis Strait	15 March — ?	J. Parker	—	30 cwt.	26
1861	Davis Strait	2 March — 5 November	W. Barron	1	1 ton	15
1862	Davis Strait	5 March — 25 October	R. Wells	2	1½ tons	28
1863	Davis Strait	3 March — 5 November	Walker	—	—	1½
1864-5	Laid up					
1866	Davis Strait	6 March — 23 October	Wm Wells	2	20 tons	16
*1867	Davis Strait	9 March — 29 October	Wm Wells	Clean	—	—
1868	Greenland	12 February — 19 August	Walker	750 seals	—	9 tons (seal oil)

* Only whaler out of Hull that year.

FURTHER READING

William Barron, *Old Whaling Days*, Hull, 1895.

Thomas Beale, *The Natural History of the Sperm Whale*, London, 1839 (second, expanded, edition).

A. G. Credland, *The 'Diana' of Hull* (Hull Museum Publications) Hull, 1979.

A. G. Credland, 'Benjamin Leigh Smith — A Forgotten Pioneer', *Polar Record*, vol. 20, no. 125, 1980, pp. 127-145.

A. G. Credland, (editor) *The Journal of Surgeon Cass aboard the Whaler 'Brunswick' of Hull, 1824* (Humberside Heritage Publications no. 18), Hull, 1988.

E. S. Dodge, *The Polar Rosses*, London, 1973.

David S. Henderson, *Fishing for the Whale*, (Dundee Museum & Art Gallery Publication no. 2) Dundee, 1977.

Philip Hepton, *William Wells, Master Mariner*, (Malet Lambert Local History Originals, vol. 7) Hull, 1982.

Philip Hepton, *Capt. Wm. Wells and the last years of the Hull Whaling Fleet 1843-69*, (Malet Lambert Local History Originals, vol. 17) Hull, 1984.

Philip Hepton, *Sailings of the Hull Whaling Fleet 1843-69* (Malet Lambert Local History Originals, vol. 14), Hull, 1985.

Gordon Jackson, *The British Whaling Trade*, London, 1978.

Basil Lubbock, *The Arctic Whalers*, Glasgow, 1937.

Leonard Harrison Matthews, *The Whale*, London, 1968.

W. Gillies Ross, *Arctic Whalers – Icy Seas*, Toronto, 1985.

William Scoresby, *An Account of the Arctic Regions*, Edinburgh, 1820.

William Scoresby, *My father*, London, 1851.

Charles Edward Smith, *From the Deep of the Sea*, London, 1922.

Christopher Thomson, *The Autobiography of an Artisan*, London, 1847.

Lyall Watson, *Sea Guide to Whales of the World*, London, 1981.

W. H. Wells, *A Voyage to the Arctic Regions*, (Malet Lambert Local History Originals, vol. 11) Hull, 1982.

William Scoresby Snr. (1760-1829).
A farmer's son from Cropton (near Pickering, Yorks.),
he first sailed on a Whitby whaler in 1785.
In 1806 he sailed in the **Resolution** *within 510 miles of the*
North Pole, reaching lat. 81°30′N.
He was also the reputed inventor of the barrel crows nest
for the whaleship's lookout. As master of the **Fame** *Scoresby*
sailed from Hull, 1820-3.

William Scoresby Jnr. (1789-1857).
Eldest son of William Scoresby Snr. he made the first
voyage with his father aged ten. He studied Chemistry,
Physics and Natural History at Edinburgh University and
his publication, **An Account of the Arctic Regions***, 1820,*
laid the foundations of modern Arctic science. He retired
from the sea in 1823 and after reading theology at
Cambridge University took holy orders and was appointed
Vicar of Bradford.

*The whaleship **Baffin**, built at Liverpool to the order of William Scoresby Jnr. in 1820,*
it was purpose designed for the Arctic fishery based on long experience in the Arctic fishery.
She was lost in 1830 sailing out of Leith under the command of Capt. Smith.
This model is displayed in the Scoresby room of the Whitby museum.

*Skeleton of the Blue Whale (Sibbald's Rorqual) (c.1906) hanging from the ceiling of the
Hull Literary and Philosophical Society's Museum in the Royal Institution, Albion Street, Hull – the "Leviathanic Museum"
referred to by Melville in **Moby Dick**. This skeleton came from the type specimen of this biggest of the whale family which was
washed up in the Humber in 1835. It measured 55ft in length when found and was first described by Dr. J. E. Gray in the
Proceedings of the Zoological Society in 1847. In 1935 it was transferred to the Natural History Museum, South Kensington,
a move which fortunately saved it from the blitz which destroyed the museum in 1943.*

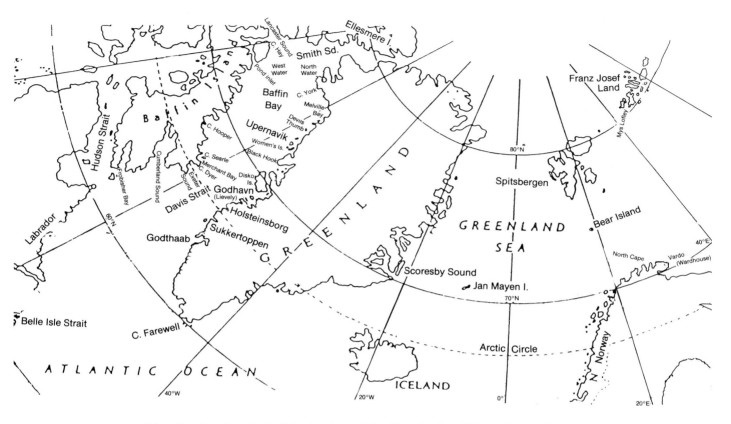

Map showing the principal destinations of the Greenland and Davis Strait whalers.